Mountain Secrets Revealed

By

Tony A. Krizan

Oakhurst, CA

Mountain Secrets Revealed

Published by:

Tony Krizan
P.O. Box 1453
Oakhurst, CA 93644
(559) 285-9243
(559) 642-6870
tonykrizan@hotmail.com

ISBN: 978-0-9897880-1-4

©2016 Tony Krizan all rights reserved.

P-40 Cover Art ©2016 Mary A. Livingston, all rights reserved, used with permission.

No Portion of this book or components may be reproduced or transmitted in any form or by any means, electronic or mechanical, including photocopying, recording, or by any informational storage and retrieval system available now or in the future, without the written permission from the author-publisher.

First Printing 2016

Dedication

It's very difficult to stumble through life and share personal successes without assistance from friends. I dedicate this book to those who shared and directed me through the trials and tribulations revealed in this book. You know who you are!

My special thanks to my favorite hiking partners, Clem Bingham and Fred Cochran, for putting up with unknown mountain canyons and trails, especially the adventures into Kings Canyon while looking for the lost Curtiss Wright P-40 fighter aircraft. Thanks to Nancy Morgan, a special person who never complained following me into the hidden canyons and washes of Death Valley. I can't forget the tireless assistance volunteered by Park Ranger Cindy Wood and her faithful mules, Rosie and Junior. Our adventures into Kings Canyon were much more enjoyable not carrying two weeks of provisions on our backs. Thanks to the knowledge of historians, Anita Fulmer, Ralph and Betty Bissett, for sharing their family's pioneering history. Thanks to those who shared their personal photos; Clem Bingham, Fred Cochran, Nancy Morgan, Hal Browder, Barbara Spillane, Bill Wagers, Phil and Sheldon Arnot.

I am also deeply grateful to the US Forest Service and the National Park Service, Oakhurst Visitors Center, Oakhurst Chamber of Commerce and Yosemite National Park Research Library for the information leading to the completion of these adventures. I can't forget the encouragement offered by Betty Linn, publisher, and Brian Wilkinson, editor, and their staff of the Sierra Star Newspaper.

Thank You!

Note from the Author

I was born on August 01, 1939 in Middletown Ohio. During that time Ohio was graced with very few roads connecting each small rural community. Many farms, woodlands, and rivers surrounded these small towns. The main source of family income was from farming, steel mills, and paper factories.

During my grade school years, I enjoyed reading books about our western frontier. The struggles of early pioneers settling the untamed west and the mystery of the Native American culture fascinated me. The Cub and Boy Scouts helped keep my interest focused on the outdoors. My favorite sports were Baseball, hiking, swimming and tennis.

At the age of 12, I established my first business, polishing aircraft at the local airport called Hook Field. Before I was fifteen, I had flown in over 35 separate aircraft. At the age of 22, I became a certified scuba diver and dove in almost every stone quarry and lake in central and southern Ohio. But my need for solitude was found in the local forests, foothills, and rivers surrounding my home.

My first 26 years were spent in Ohio. In 1965 I moved my wife, Janice, and daughters, Diane and Donna, to Southern California looking to settle into the Golden State that I read about while growing up. Lockheed Aircraft hired me as a General Machinist, which was my trade at that time. I advanced to working for Kelly Johnson whose department was commonly known as the Skunk Works. Through my productive years within the workplace, I advanced into sales and management with companies in the Southern California area. I continued my education at Los Angeles City College.

In 1978 I met Tom "Silver Fox" Addison. His forty-plus years hiking the Sierra Nevada Mountains channeled my desire to rekindle those memories of the wilderness surrounding my home in Ohio. With his professional skills of the Sierra Nevada Wilderness, it focused me into the mysteries surrounding these California Mountains. In the following decades, I completed over 75 major hikes, some solo, and four times that amount day hiking. Yosemite, Kings Canyon National Parks, Ansel Adams, John Muir, and Kaiser Wilderness are a few areas I've hiked locally. Ohio, Kentucky, Colorado, Arizona, and Oregon also share special places in my hiking memories.

I presently write for the Sierra Star Newspaper in Oakhurst California sharing my adventures in the Sierra Nevada Mountains. I also feature my personal hiking experiences while offering slide show presentations to the public. My personal library contains wilderness photos and history dating back to the early pioneering years of California.

Tony Krizan

Contents

Dedication	iii
Note from the Author	iv
First P-40 Search	1
Second P-40 Search	12
Third P-40 Search	20
Passage through the Minarets	25
Minaret Mine Trek	29
Trekking through the Minarets	33
Return to the Snaffle Bit Trail	41
Snaffle Bit Tree, where are you?	44
Treasures of Death Valley	47
Treasures of Death Valley	53
Death Valley's Darwin Falls	57
Death Valley's Panamint Dunes	62
Death Valley Fall Canyon	65
Death Valley Marble Canyon	70
Forgotten Wawona Stagecoach Road	75
High Sierra Route	89
North Lake, Piute Pass and Beyond	95
Surprises at Puppet Pass and LaSalle Lake	99
Feather Pass to Lake Italy	103
Mystery of Cox Col Pass	107
Detour into Mountain History	111
History along the Mono Trail	115
P-40 Fourth of Fifth Found	119

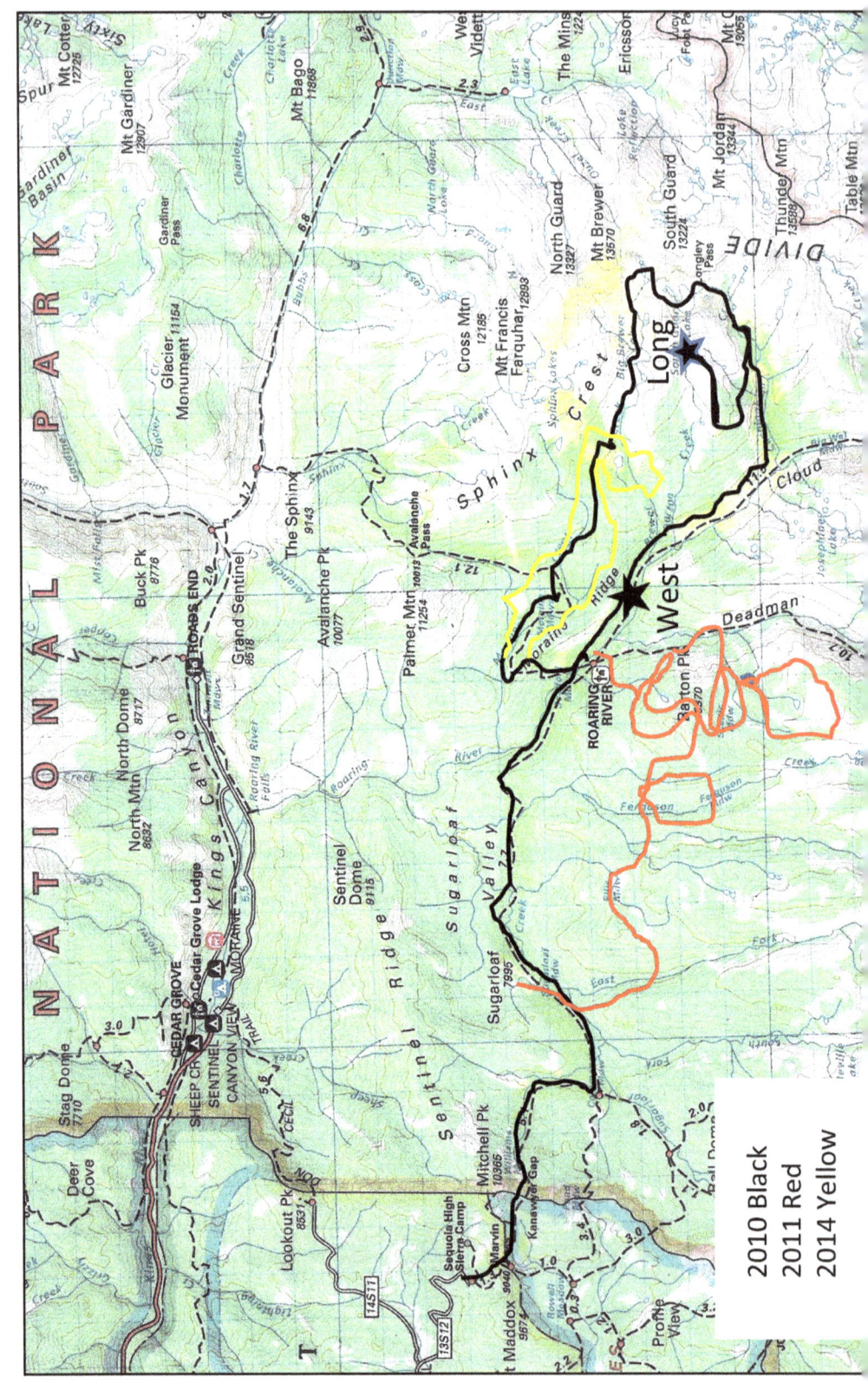

One
First P-40 Search
Sometime in 1949

Could it be one single event in one's life that alters the decisions made five decades into the future? Sometimes it's impossible to recognize influential events because the lack of education or importance at the time of discovery. As a young boy growing up next to an airport in Southern Ohio, aircraft fascinated me. I can't remember a day that aircraft flying overhead wouldn't distract me from everyday responsibilities. Over time, I could identify each model aircraft by their distinctive markings or the sound of their pulsating engine.

One memorable day, during the summer of 1949, after finishing my Saturday morning chores around the family home, I passed the time of day looking at aviation photos and reading articles on aviation. One featured a flight of P-40 Curtiss Wright Fighter Aircraft that were on a training mission in California. The P-40 aircraft fascinated me because it was the aircraft Major General Clair Lee Chennault and his American Volunteer Group (AVG) made famous defending the Chinese border before WW2. They called this group of aviators "Flying Tigers".

The story stated that on October 24, 1941, nineteen P-40 Tomahawk aircraft departed from March Air Force Base in Riverside California on a two-hour flight to McClellan Air Field outside of Sacramento California. Somehow they became confused with their flight direction and surprisingly found themselves over the heart of the

Tony A. Krizan

Sierra Nevada Mountains. Problems developed with the aircraft and five of the P-40's crashed in and around Kings Canyon National Park.

At the time I read the article on the nineteen P-40's, I didn't know it would become part of my future. Due to my fascination of WW2 aircraft, this story crossed my path many times through conversations and articles of historic moments of early aviation. One day in 2004, I read another article entitled; A Bad Command Decision by the author Don L. Jordon. This was the same story but more involved in details and added history about the five crashed aircraft and their pilots.

Was this an omen awakening me and centering my attention on this lost flight? I asked myself qualifying questions: Why does this story keep occupying part of my waking hours year after year? Why did I move to California years ago from Ohio? Why did I move from Southern California to the small mountain town of Oakhurst? And why did I, after all these years, keep hiking the majestic Sierra Nevada Mountains?

Could I have subconsciously accepted the challenge to solve the mystery of that one lost remaining aircraft? The Curtiss Wright P-40 Tomahawk Fighter Aircraft #39-194 was flown by Lieutenant Leonard C. Lydon of the 57 Pursuit Squadron based in Windsor Locks Connecticut. His aircraft was one of five that crashed. During the past decades, four of the aircraft were located, but Lieutenant Lydon's bird still remained a mystery.

After a few years of researching information posted by qualified authors and hikers, it was time for me to put my wilderness talents to use. I set up my personal expedition with the help of my two buddies, Clem Bingham, and Fred Cochran. First, we eliminated the areas previously searched over the past six decades. We reasoned that after six decades, someone would've tripped over this crash site with all the human traffic of hikers, packers, fisherman, trappers, and even cowboys chasing grazing cattle. I'm not ruling out private and commercial aircraft that have participated in this search. Our objective was to search the areas overlooked by concerned individuals.

Over the years my hiking partners, Clem and Fred, shared many of my past journeys into the wilderness. Lucky for me they also enjoyed new adventures, so when I presented them with this new unknown, they were hesitant at first, but after a few weeks of pointing out the positives, they approved!

On July 28, 2010, we departed from the Marvin Pass Trailhead at 8,360 feet. We started a thirteen day hiking adventure into Kings Canyon. Our objective was to relocate and photograph the crash sites of three of the five P-40's. After communicating with the National Park Service, they volunteered the locations of Lieutenant Jack C. West and Lieutenant Richard N. Long's crash sites.

Our first day we climbed to 9,080 feet, then descended the long and winding trail to Comanche Meadow at 8,060 feet for our first camp. A few of Kings Canyon's campsites were equipped with bear-boxes, a welcome addition to hiding food from the native Black Bears. The following morning along this remote trail were the tracks of one of these local residents from the night before. Lucky for us, he continued moving down the trail.

Later that afternoon the Sugar Loaf and Ferguson Creeks were both a challenge with their swift-moving water. The crossing at Sugar Loaf Creek forced us to remove our boots and roll up our pants before crossing. We hiked another two miles before arriving at Ferguson Creek. Upstream from this trail junction a tree had fallen across to the opposite bank. With a test of our balancing skills, this old snag offered a dry crossing.

The trail increased in elevation as we finally reached the saddle where the valley opened up with views of Palmer Mountain. (Directly behind is the towering mountain formation called the Sphinx Mountain Range. Off in the distance to the east was the Great Western Divide sharing its snow run-off into the Roaring River directly below us. We dropped in elevation following the trail along the Roaring River another three miles before reaching the ranger station. Before arriving at the station, we passed an old geological survey cabin built sometime during the early 1900's. This 15x20 log cabin had fallen victim to an avalanche that crushed the roof. The strong side walls were still standing upright. Our next campsite was located next to the Roaring River Ranger Station.

The following morning we set out to photograph the P-40 (#39-285) crash site of Lieutenant Jack C. West. From previous research, we expected to locate his aircraft almost a half mile from the ranger station, south of the Dead Man Canyon Trail. After nearly two hours searching, there was no sign of the wreckage. After 69 years, perhaps someone removed and cleaned up this crash site.

It was late afternoon when we returned to camp. While we were gone the head park ranger, Cindy Wood arrived back to her post bringing in supplies. During an enlightening conversation with Cindy, she explained to us that she knew of a wreck site just over a half mile following the Cloud Canyon Trail. The crash site was located across the river. We planned to follow her directions the next morning and maybe we would find West's aircraft.

With our new directions, we set out the following morning. The area south of Cloud Canyon Trail was our next search. The melting snowpack increased the Roaring River to a dangerous level. We walked downstream a short distance and found a logjam extending across the river. After another balancing act on narrow logs, we completed our task arriving at the south bank without getting wet. Less than 40 yards from the river, a metallic reflection from the sun identified the site of Lieutenant Wests P-40 aircraft.

Pieces of debris were piled up at two locations. An impact crater still remained with the rusted propeller and spinner resting within the deep scar. I was surprised at the amount of wreckage scattered throughout the area, probably caused by the explosion on impact. Just outside the crater were the remains of the engine, manifold, crankshaft, and pistons. They were twisted and crushed almost beyond recognition. Even after 69 years some of the aluminum pieces still had the original olive drab paint. Lieutenant West bailed out and survived this crash without injuries. Many thanks to Cindy for her directions to this wreck site! Just for history records, the GPS coordinates were 36 degrees 42,246N and 118 degrees 34,578W at elevation 7,744 feet. These numbers were not available at the National Park Service.

During the year of 1989, with the permission of the park service, Operation Tomahawk led by Pat Mocha and Kent Lentz confiscated

Wreckage from Lt. Jack C West's crash site.

Lt. Jack C. West's crash site with Tony Krizan,
Fred Cochran and Clem Bingham holding the P-40 prop.

most of the larger usable parts from this site. They were carried out by packhorses or helicopter. The parts were used to restore another P-40 Tomahawk Aircraft. History reveals that P-40#284 was the only flying survivor from that fateful day when the Imperial Japanese War Machine bombed Pearl Harbor on December 07, 1941.

Following that find, we headed back to the ranger station to pack up our gear and relocate and photograph Lieutenant Richard N. Long's P-40 crash site. We hiked the Cloud Canyon Trail to the junction of Cunningham Creek. As we followed this trail, Brewer and Barton Creek gave us another reason to remove our boots. Surprising how much water flows in these mountain streams. Once at Cunningham Creek, looking at its angle of elevation we realized the difficulty we'd face following this creek. With no trail, we maneuvered through thick Manzanita bushes and lush ground cover concealing deep crevasses while bolder hopping.

Two miles and seven hours later, we arrived at 10,600 feet. The GPS quadrants given to us stated that Lieutenant Long's wreck site was located at this elevation. After searching over two hours, I questioned if I had the correct information. Perhaps the quadrants were incorrect like those first given to us for the Lieutenant West crash site. Maybe they meant 11,600 feet instead of 10,600 feet. Once again, we started climbing in elevation following the creek another half mile before setting up camp. After a full day of wreck searching, evening was rapidly approaching.

The next morning we continued our search using the secondary numbers from another map. While climbing, I found a discarded helium balloon colored in bright blue, red, and silver with the inscription, Happy Birthday. Sometimes a personal gift happens by surprise even within the wilderness. I accepted the gift from the mountains because the previous day was my birthday.

From this elevation, I could see the resemblance of a whale's back extending upward from the valley to an elevation of 11,726 feet. This distant mountain was named Whale Back Mountain by the USGS during the 1903 survey for the Tehipite 30' map on its first edition in 1905.

Totally exhausted from searching along Cunningham Creek, we set up camp around 11,100 feet. The next day we'd use our only remaining tool to help locate the wreck site, a photo taken in 1989 by Operation Tomahawk. With the photo they took of the wreck-site we hoped to triangulate mountain peaks and line up the area of its location.

We climbed to 11,300 feet for an over-all view of the valley and surrounding mountains. We realized after comparing the photo with the surrounding area, Cunningham Creek drainage was the wrong canyon. Using triangulation revealed a mountain to climb over between the wreck site and us. Totally exhausted from the day's search, we spent another night at 11,100 feet.

The next morning we planned a descent down the creek to look for a safe route around the west side of the drainage and hoped there was a canyon behind the mountain. It wasn't necessary to break up our campsite because we'd have to hike back through this canyon to reach the saddle over Cinder Col Pass at 12,172 feet.

It was another beautiful morning with the sun cresting over the eastern ridge chasing the shadows back into hiding. The shadows remained hidden until the sun settled behind the western ridge that evening. Now was time for us to backtrack two miles to the questionable canyon west of the drainage. We were fortunate most of the snow patches had melted on the eastern slope. It was late morning before we located the hidden canyon and followed its run-off stream into its interior. Before splitting up to search this canyon I double-checked the photo with the map and surrounding mountains. All the triangulation points lined up, so we started our search.

At 11,517 feet within the center of the canyon, we found the wreckage of Lieutenant Richard N. Long's P-40 aircraft. The force of the impact was so severe that the engine block was split. All three prop blades were twisted and bent but still attached to the hub. The pistons and crankshaft were distorted with pieces of the aircraft scattered around the area. Similar to the Lieutenant West crash-site at the Roaring River almost all the aircraft parts were removed in 1989.

Pat Mocha of Operation Tomahawk erected a rock memorial at the site. Tucked inside the memorial was a cylinder with a note describing the location and the pilot's identification.

Lt. Richard N Long's crash site with Tony Krizan,
Fred Cochran and Clem Bingham holding the P-40 prop.

Lieutenant Richard N Long from the 57th Pursuit Group, a Curtiss Wright P-40 #39-287 crashed on October 24, 1941.

We dated and signed the back of the note and replaced it inside the cylinder. We restacked the memorial stones, lowered our heads, and took a few moments of silence before we departed. The GPS coordinates were 36 degrees 41,325N and 118 degrees 30,509W at elevation 11,517 feet.

Even at this extreme elevation, a Humming Bird was curious about us and buzzed the red bandana Fred had tied around his neck. The high mountains were still displaying wildflowers, so maybe this was what attracted the Humming Birds.

Finally, after seven days, we located Lieutenant Richard N Long's P-40 aircraft. What a rewarding feeling after all of our trial and errors, and to think an old photograph was the catalyst that opened the pathway to the location. After completing our photography, we started our journey back to our campsite at 11,100 feet. I looked forward to getting a good night's rest and hoped to be well rested for the next few

Memorial and engine from Lt. Richard N Long crash site.

days while looking for Lieutenant Leonard C. Lydon's P-40 #39-194 hidden somewhere in Kings Canyon National Park.

The next morning we followed Cunningham Creek to its headwaters at South Guard Lake at 11,760 feet. While climbing around its east side, we forged through patches of snow from the previous winter. With the lack of trees at that elevation, it was much easier visually searching the small rock canyons. We passed in front of South Guard Peak at 13,224 feet and Mount Brewer at 13,570 feet. Off in the distance was the snow-covered ridge that was hiding our highest saddle called Cinder Col Pass at 12,172 feet.

Over five feet of snow was still remaining at the pass. A dangerous slope tapered down the opposite side. This obstacle forced us to climb to a higher elevation to bypass the problem. We climbed up and over class three obstacles. With a full pack, negotiating some of the huge rock formations, ropes would have added safety. However the plan change was successful so we could start our descent to Big Brewer Lake at 10.961 feet for our next campsite.

Big Brewer Lake was another large mountain lake with steep sloping side canyons ideal for hiding the remains of any aircraft. Throughout the day's trek with the help of my field glasses, I searched the canyon walls and rock formations looking for a shape or reflection from an aged aluminum skin. Once again, we completed another day of searching and I was looking forward to crawling into a warm sleeping bag for a good night's sleep. Nature provided us with a beautiful sunset. The mountains surrounding us turned bright orange just before the shadows of dark surrounded us.

The next morning we descended to Little Brewer Lake at 9,735 feet for our next campsite. After four days searching above the tree line, the addition of trees within these adjoining canyons nearly eliminated the use of field glasses. Fred and Clem climbed and searched the canyons and ridges on the lake's east side. I ventured up to a shelf on the west side. Once again, I became excited when the narrow shelf opened up into a large canyon. I spent over two hours crossing from one canyon to another. The darkness of evening was rapidly approaching when I started boulder hopping to the summits to view those hidden areas shielded by the dense forest. Fantastic views of the valley we had just hiked earlier in the morning and great views of the valley and canyons behind the shelf. It was almost 8:00 p.m. when I returned to camp. I hoped my buddies had good news because I struck out; no P-40 aircraft! They were also disappointed with their wilderness search.

The next morning we decided to change our departure route from following the Moraine Ridge at 8,000 feet to intersect Avalanche Trail. Instead, we struck out in an alternate direction and followed the 9,000-foot ridge to the west and hiked through another dense part of the huge forest. If we couldn't locate the aircraft we could try to locate one of Shorty Loveless' fourteen log cabins. Shorty Loveless was a trapper that made his living in these mountains from 1910 to 1952 in the dead of winter trapping for fur pelts.

The foliage during this three-mile cross-country adventure was very dense with many downed trees, which made for slow trekking. In past adventures, we found two of Shorty's cabins. This day, no cabin or aircraft were located along this route change. We located the Avalanche

Barton Lackey wilderness cabin. The location Lt. Jack West and Leonard Lyden met after crashing in Kings Canyon National Park and survived snow storm.

Trail to lead us back to the Roaring River Ranger Station. Both the cabin and aircraft were still a mystery.

Speaking of log cabins, after Lieutenants West and Lydon bailed out of their P-40 aircrafts, they located a log cabin and managed to survive eight days before they were rescued. I wondered if that log cabin was still standing? The magazine article stated it was located in a meadow next to the Roaring River. At the Roaring River Ranger Station, we crossed the bridge and proceeded downstream. Less than 10 minutes following a trail, a log structure came into view. The Barton Lackey Cabin still existed! It was still livable but was primarily used for storage.

After thirteen days and over 47 miles of searching, we arrived back to our trailhead. Who would think a vehicle would look so inviting? I looked forward to traveling for the next few miles in the sitting position.

Two
Second P-40 Search
August 07, 2011

A year had passed since our first attempt to locate that fallen Curtiss Wright P-40 aircraft flown by Lieutenant Leonard C. Lydon. Hidden somewhere in Kings Canyon National Park was #39-194, a fighter aircraft belonging to the 57 Pursuit Squadron based out of Windsor Locks Air Field in Connecticut. Was it possible that the mountains around Kings Canyon would surprise us and release this 70-year-old mystery?

First, let me give you a brief history of what originated this dramatic event. During early October 1941 Congress needed verification that our Army Air Force could defend the United States from a foreign aggressor. They chose the 57 Pursuit Squadron based out of Windsor Lock Connecticut. Their mission was to fly a series of hops across the United States to test their defensive capabilities. Of the 25 aircraft departing from Windsor Locks Air Field, only 19 arrived at March Army Air Base in Riverside California. Six aircraft had mechanical problems and were grounded along their flight plan. The following day 19 aircraft departed for McClellan Field outside of Sacramento for their first fueling stop. Their final destination was to be McCord Air Field outside of Settle Washington.

Even with an early snowstorm warning over the Sierra Nevada Mountains, Major Clayton Hughes, their squadron leader, ignored the weather bulletin. He believed his flight would be south of the storm by following the San Joaquin Valley to Sacramento California.

Major Hughes became disoriented along the flight plan and found his squadron of 19 aircraft directly over the Sierra Nevada Mountains. He was flying almost 50 miles off course to the east between mountains above 14,000 feet. He ordered his squadron to increase their elevation to 17,000 feet. Early aircraft weren't equipped with oxygen, and their carburetor deicing devices were wired open for increased flight mileage. With the thinner air and colder temperatures the carburetors froze and the engines shut down. Three pilots bailed out and survived. Two remained with their aircraft and perished.

After spending the winter researching maps of Kings Canyon and focusing our attention south of the Roaring River, we decided to search the area surrounding Barton Peak. Research revealed that an abandoned trail, forgotten for over 30 years, followed from the Sugar Loaf Creek behind Barton Peak. Our hike started once again from the Marvin Pass trailhead. Our first night was spent at the Sugar Loaf camp next to the Sugar Loaf Creek. The beginning of that forgotten trail crossed the creek at our camping area. We hoped it would lead us to Ferguson Creek and the back side of Barton Peak.

Forest Ranger Cindy Wood offered the usage of her two pack mules, Junior and Rosie, to carry our supplies to our first base camp at Ferguson Creek. Two weeks of provisions can become quite heavy resting upon one's back. Once we crossed the creek, the mules found the abandoned trail. Fred, Clem, and I were on foot. Following their hoof prints made our trek much easier.

There were a couple of setbacks with the mules. A steep area through the rocks on a hillside caused one of the trailing horses to panic. When the horse panicked, it pulled the other animals off-balance. Three of the six animals went tumbling down the hillside with our supplies. Luckily they survived with only bruises. We lost over an hour repacking the mules and the same amount of time convincing them to travel over the same route. Before reaching the top of this plateau, the same skittish horse broke loose and decided to run back down the

Cindy Wood with her stock packing in our supplies to Ellis Meadow in Kings Canyon.

mountain. After a short foot race, I managed to catch him, and we joined the remaining pack. They took to calling me, Cowboy Tony.

Once over the saddle, we were greeted by an unexpected surprise. An unnamed creek took us more than an hour to cross. Again, downed trees and thick vegetation made travel difficult for the livestock. With the time lost from animal behavior and cutting our way through dead trees and limbs, we had to set up camp early at Ellis Meadow at 8,010 feet. Time and daylight were our concern even though we were roughly three-quarters of a mile from our designated campsite. The meadow made an excellent place to set up camp that evening.

Another clear August morning but the temperature was dipping to the freezing mark. Once again, we had problems locating the trail, so we chose an alternate route cross-country trying to locate the path to Ferguson Creek West. Then the impossible happened, the terrain became too difficult for the stock. Cindy turned back, returning to Sugar Loaf Trail with the stock. This forced us to carry our heavy supplies to our designated base camp nearly a half mile away.

It took us almost three hours forging our way through the thick brush before locating an area by the creek to set up camp. Over the next two days, we managed to search the canyons and ridges on the south side of Ferguson Creek.

After further examination of our map, we decided to relocate our camp to the base of Barton Peak. This move would give us easier access to the small canyons below the mountain. With the intention of returning to Ferguson Creek camp for another night, we set out looking for an easy route to the mountain base.

As we hiked through the thick underbrush, East Ferguson Creek appeared. Fred paused, turned to me and stated that this was the same area he and his wife, Peggy, sat on a log and fed dried peas to the native trout back in 1986. Then for further verification, we hiked downstream 30 yards and found the forgotten trail. We found memories, but no aircraft.

Upstream was a natural logjam, we used for a natural stream crossing. After a half hour struggling to maneuver through a wet meadow, finally at 8,800 feet, our future campsite came into view. We got lucky, a large flat area with tree cover and a small seasonal stream at its northern boundary. On our return to camp, we continued our searching the west side of this huge meadow.

After relocating at our new camp, our search continued through two remote canyons increasing in elevation to 9,200 feet. These canyons revealed a few old markers, possibly from the cattle or sheepherders during the early twentieth century. The next day we'd search at a higher elevation and horizontally trek along the base of Barton Peak.

Morning temperature at base camp 2 was much warmer at 45 degrees compared to 34 degrees along Ferguson Creek. We planned to hike three abreast within shouting distance searching the canyons and ridges horizontally on the west side of Barton Peak. By afternoon, we arrived at a natural pond on the north face at 9,500 feet. Then we continued back across the northwest face again at 9,100 feet back to base camp. Seven hours of searching revealed no aircraft.

The following morning we angled up the west side of Barton Peak until we reached the summit at 10,379 feet. From that location field glasses aided in scanning the hidden areas concealed at the lower elevations. Great views to the north and within an eight-mile radius were

From 12,100 foot ridge, Barton Peak, Scenic Meadow and Palmer Mountain.

the areas we searched last year: Palmer Mountain, Sphinx Crest, Mount Brewer, South Guard Peak and the Cunningham Creek Drainage. To the northeast, in the distance was the Great Western Divide.

The top of Barton Peak was very gentle with a few Pine Trees and interesting rock formations. On its east side, below us was Scenic Meadow. That would be the location of our next base camp if the P-40 aircraft failed to appear.

On our descent, after a few rest stops, Fred discovered he misplaced his water bottle and camera. Lucky Fred had his GPS and I still had my faithful compass that has been my companion since my childhood as a Cub Scout. We retraced our footsteps the following morning and within 45 minutes found his gear lying next to a boulder where we rested the previous afternoon.

After four days searching Barton Peak, we tried to locate the only trail (not shown on any map) called the Barton, Lackey Elevator Trail. This was the only trail leading up the peak from the Roaring River used by early cowboys to check on their cattle at the higher elevation meadows. If we couldn't find the old trail, it was possible we'd have to double back to the original unmaintained trail leading to Sugar Loaf Creek. We'd heard that cattleman, Al Lackey, carved the Barton, Lackey Elevator Trail up the mountain in 1945. Keep in mind that the trail may have been removed by natural occurrences of erosion and time. When our map revealed we were in the general area, we followed a natural drainage channel. Luck was with us again; we found trail markers that led us to this steep and challenging trail. In five days we'd be back to follow it down to the Roaring River Ranger Station.

We arrived back to base camp early enough to pack up and hike over the 10,000-foot saddle to Scenic Meadow for our third and final camp. Another surprise; while we were hiking through a remote canyon I discovered an original Indian trail marker, a huge boulder weighing over 170 pounds. It was placed on top of another huge boulder. I stopped and visually scanned the area surrounding this marker. There was no way this rock could've tumbled down and come to rest at this point, and the melting of snow couldn't have chosen the location for the rock's final resting place. Years ago my mentor who taught me the secrets of hiking these mountains, Tom (Silver Fox) Addison a mountain man with over 50 years hiking experience, introduced to me the physical examples of this type of marker. If we found two or three identical markers leading in a logical direction, it could be a historical marker. So I started searching and in less than 50 feet I located another 150 pound plus rock and 50 feet beyond this marker was another. What was interesting about the find was it was following the same direction toward the saddle to Scenic Meadow. I believe our American Indians were at this location first.

The trek over the saddle was much steeper than expected, so we created our own switchback trails for an elevation gain of 1,200 feet. I was impressed by the rock formations adding interest to this saddle. Where these natural formations formed by water erosion or was this area was under water millions of years ago?

Just like its name, the picturesque location Scenic Meadow introduced itself with two streams gently flowing through its location. One stream followed its eastern border and the other flowed through

From Barton Peak looking east toward higher ridge above Scenic Meadow.

the center. Waving in the breeze above the green grass were wild flowers with colors of white, yellow, and purple. I believed we were going to enjoy this location. While looking around, we realized that this area had been occupied by one of the local inhabits. Less than 20 yards from our campsite was the sleeping quarters of a native Black Bear. Fortunate for us, this bear didn't return while we were there.

Looking to the east, a ridge extending almost a half-mile long and over 11,000 feet in elevation would be our next destination. From this advantage point, we could overlook the east side of Barton Peak and the canyon south of the high ridge. Getting to the top would be a challenge for us; we had no idea that two sections of these areas were class 3. After some struggling, we reached the ridge and opted to check out the north face first as it dropped over 3,000 feet into the canyon below. In the distance across the canyon, I could see the no name canyon where Lieutenant Longs P-40 crashed. Mountain climbers, Phil and Sheldon Arnot, on July 07, 1959 first discovered Long's wreckage while mountain climbing the eastern ridge below South Guard Lake.

We followed this no name ridge to the South and hiked to the summit at 11,169 feet. As we forged closer to the summit, periodically we would pause and with the help of our field glasses scan the surrounding area. It was possible the crash site may not resemble an aircraft, so we would look for any object out of place or possibly a reflection from its metal skin or windshield. Once again, another full day of searching and no sign of the missing P-40 aircraft.

Two days remained, so we searched the northeast ridges and face of Barton Peak. We summited another mountain shelf to 10,050 feet and searched the overgrown canyons and forests. Once again, no aircraft! But we did find a 20-foot white quartz vein extending up the mountain 80 feet.

On our final day, we decided once again to hike through the forest and canyons to the northeast of our base camp. After six hours we arrived back at our camp. Our silence revealed the disappointment felt not solving the seven-decade-old mystery.

We hiked out the following day by doubling back across the saddle, through the remote canyons to the Elevator Trail. While following our route that morning, high within the treetops, a hawk squawked us while flying from tree to tree. Maybe we were much too close to its nest or she didn't approve of intruders walking through her territory. After forging our way through the heavy brush, we located the drainage route and the trail markers we found five days earlier. Steep was a gentle word for this forgotten and dangerous path. Ropes would've been a confidence booster during our descent. We had no choice but take our time using handholds knowing this was the only route descending to the Roaring River Ranger Station.

We took a full day to rest and shared our findings with Cindy Wood, the head Park Ranger. She was overwhelmed listening to highlights of an area that was on her list to explore in the future. The following morning we started our 14-mile hike back to the Marvin Pass Trailhead. After 16 days and 52 miles of hiking these remote mountains, our searching area was complete for the summer of 2011.

Three
Third P-40 Search
July 20, 2014

Three years passed since I was in Kings Canyon looking for Lieutenant Leonard C. Lydon P-40 aircraft that crashed on October 24, 1941. Once again through the winter months, I studied maps hoping to find a logical crash area and discover the reason why no one had located this aircraft to date. With California suffering through its fourth year of drought, maybe the areas with less ground cover and a sparse mountain snowpack would expose his aircraft.

Two of the five pilots that I haven't introduced yet are Lieutenants John H. Pease and William H. Burrell. Lieutenant John H. Pease was first to bail out and survived around the Wildrose Meadow area about 5 miles north of Kennedy Meadows. His aircraft also suffered an engine failure, crashed and was removed from the site two weeks later. Lieutenant Pease walked to a ranch house and contacted authorities. The original ranch owners have passed away, but their children stated that the crash site's exact location was unknown to them.

Before introducing my book for printing I received two important additions to this story. Lieutenant Pease retired as a Colonel and he is celebrating his 97th year of life in Colorado. On June 18, 2016 a lone hiker, Jonathan Beck, was trekking solo off trail and stumbled across an aircraft crash site. After reviewing his photos; he

Tony at Lieutenant William H. Burrell's crash site
on Grays Mountain above Bass Lake.

may have rediscovered Colonel John H. Pease's P-40 wreckage. With joint identification from two seasoned researchers, Pat Macha and Kent Lentz we agreed this was the only P-40 from records that crashed in this general area. Hiker stated; he abandoned the Haiwee Trail and opted for a short cut toward the South Fork of the Kern River and he stumbled across an aircraft crash site.

We planned a hike for September 24, 2016 into the remote area of Kern Plateau to photograph and verify this aircraft. We strongly believed this was Colonel John H. Pease's P-40. Which would mean that only one P-40 remained a mystery and was hidden somewhere in Kings Canyon National Park.

Lieutenant William H. Burrell was the last to crash. In a blinding snowstorm, he flew through Kings Canyon and blindly managed to dodge the high elevation peaks before entering the Bass Lake area. His flight came to an abrupt halt when he flew directly into Grays Mountain around 5,840 feet and lost his life. Today a memorial plaque and part of an engine rest at that location. His quadrants were Latitude 37 degrees 24,36 minutes, Longitude 119 degrees 32,30 minutes.

Tony and Clem next to the cabin of Shorty Loveless,
a fur trapper from 1910 to 1951 in Kings Canyon.

On July 20, 2014, the three of us stood at the Marvin Pass Trailhead. Once again we were patiently waiting to start our eight-day adventure into Kings Canyon. We hiked nine miles to Sugar Loaf Camp for the first night. There we met up with Park Ranger Cindy Wood and her pack mules carrying our supplies. The following morning we departed at first light hiking across Sugar Loaf and Ferguson Creeks down to the trail that followed the Roaring River.

During our first hike, following this river trail in 2010, we stumbled into a forgotten survivor's log cabin. During the four years that followed, nature decided to physically change this retreating cabin by dropping a huge dying pine tree upon its structure. It must be true that over time nature will take back what she generously gives us. Next, we intersected the Avalanche Trail after crossing the Roaring River and hiked north climbing in elevation over the Moraine Ridge. Hoping the stock packing our gear didn't overtake us before we started our cross-country trek east toward Little Brewer Lake.

I previously mentioned a fur trapper named Shorty Loveless whose log cabin we searched for before locating the Avalanche Trail. He trapped this area of Kings Canyon from 1910 to 1952. Cindy stated she knew the location of that cabin north of Moraine Ridge and east of Moraine Creek. Our wait wasn't long before Cindy arrived. On foot, we followed Cindy, who was leading the stock carrying our supplies. Twenty minutes later we crossed Moraine Creek and were forging our way through the brush. Less than 100 yards from the creek was Shorty's cabin snuggled between two huge boulders. In 2010, while searching for Lydon's aircraft, we passed within 200 feet of this cabin. A testament to the thick foliage in these mountains!

We started our final climb following the ridge and increased in elevation another 1,300 feet. Following our map, we arrived at a small no-name lake, then skirted around to the east side and continued into the next canyon. Using a compass reading, we hiked northeast to Little Brewer Lake. If it weren't for my map and compass, I would still be wondering around those mountains. It was an extremely long day after departing Sugar Loaf Campsite at 7:45 a.m. We arrived at our base camp at 7:30 p.m. Total elevation gain for the day was 2,485 feet.

Sitting around the campsite that evening and heating up freeze dried food was a real treat, compared to the fruit, nuts and cheese during the day. In 2010 we explored this remote area around Little Brewer Lake. To the east behind this 11,000-foot ridge was our destination to search for the next four days.

The next morning we followed the Brewer Creek run-off down to 9,100 feet searching the eastern mountainside. We contoured around the mountain toward the remote area of the Barton Creek drainage. After five hours of searching, we decided to return back to our base camp. Not often do we stumble across abandoned trail markers, but while hiking up a drainage slot from Barton Creed there was a series of three markers. This caused me to wonder who and when these stacked rocks were placed. I followed them for a short distance but branched off into my own route. We arrived back to camp with time to spare to just relax and enjoy the auburn colored evening sunset reflecting off the lake.

Roaring River Ranger Station in Kings Canyon.

That evening after dinner, my back started giving me problems. This was confusing to me because in my 33 years of hiking, I've never had a physical hiking problem. After a serious discussion with Fred and Clem, we took into consideration after looking at our map, our location with its distance from any outside help. The ranger station was five miles away, with almost four of those miles being cross-country. There were another 14 miles by trails from the ranger station to the trailhead. With these statistics, our decision was to pack up the following morning and hike back to the ranger station to let me recuperate for a couple of days. This resting time helped, but the back pain persisted. Sad to say we departed the next morning for the trailhead.

Lieutenant Leonard C. Lydon's P-40 aircraft was still a mystery. But on the positive side, there was always another year, and maybe 2015 or 2016 will be the year that this 74-year-old mystery is solved.

Four
Passage through the Minarets
August 04, 2012

I've always wondered what the terrain was like surrounding the Minaret Mountains. Steve Roper's book, High Sierra Route, introduced me to hidden passages within the Sierra Nevada Mountains. There are rough unidentified trails throughout the mountains, but following some of these trails can limit one from experiencing choice areas contained within his book. After sharing a few years of research with hiking buddies, Clem Bingham and Fred Cochran, we decided in August of 2012 to attempt a loop starting on the west side of the Minarets. Then continue toward the east side, following the Minaret Range north before crossing back over the top to complete the loop. We estimated this hiking adventure to be 47 miles and 10 days with elevations from 6,300 feet to 13,143 feet.

On August 04, 2012 we gathered up our hiking gear to experience this new adventure into the Sierra Nevada Mountains. Our early morning departure was from the Mammoth Trailhead at 7,495 feet located beyond the town of North Fork toward Clover Meadow. Sheep Crossing at 6,300 feet was our first junction area. This crossing was made famous long before the sheepherders entered these mountains during the late 1800's. The American Indians used this lower elevation route for centuries trading with their eastern brothers.

After climbing in elevation past Snake Meadow, we had difficulty locating a flat area close to water for our first campsite.

John Becks cabin, photo taken in 1938 with Lee Verret standing in photo. Cabin built around 1882. Photo from Verret collection, used with permission.

Generally, late in the summer season, most seasonal streams dry up. Finally at Cargyle Creek, which still had a small stream of water, an old abandoned campsite was located. Who would believe that during the drought summer it would rain? But by one a.m. the rain stopped, and the following morning we continued our adventure.

The Forest Ranger at Clover Meadow Ranger Station stated, "Don't be surprised with the trail conditions. The trail crews have been working overtime clearing downed timber from the trails." He estimated 50 trees still remained blocking the mountain trails. I quit counting after climbing over and estimated 35 downed trees. This was the aftermath of that catastrophic storm of November 30 and December 01 of 2011. The USFS had cut over 500 fallen trees clearing these mountain trails.

Our second campsite was at Fern Lake snuggled within a forested canyon at 8,774 feet. From above the lake, I could see the shallow shelves just a few feet below the lake's surface offering a reflective color change in the water. The three hiking fishermen we met at the lake can testify that the fishing was great!

The following morning we switched to a new trail that climbed in elevation leading to Beck's Cabin at 9,000 feet. After many decades all that remained of his cabin was the rock fireplace and a few logs

Minaret Lake below mountain, photo from Nancy Pass.

from its lower foundation. John Beck was a gold miner and named two mountain lakes after himself around 1882. He had a prospecting mine at the outlet of the lower lake. He was also one of the early owners of the Minaret Mines located on the south slope of Iron Mountain.

After following a somewhat used trail leading to Superior Lake at 9,220 feet, it opened up to a beautiful valley surrounded by trees with a view extending down to the San Joaquin River.

Next we were faced with climbing over 10,200 feet to Nancy's Pass with no trail and a slope covered with scree (small gravel) and talus (large boulders). The pass was named after Nancy Scanlon, who climbed its slope in 1967 at the age of eight and sadly died of cancer two years later.

After a brutal three hours of climbing, we arrived at the summit of the ridge. Off in the distance, to the east were the ragged peaks of the Minarets. Directly below the peaks was our first view of the Minaret Lake, only two days of hiking away. First we descended another mile to a small run-off pond (tarn) below Dead Horse Lake for our next campsite at 9,280 feet. This ideal setting was located within a cluster of Tamarac Pines overlooking the tarn overshadowed by the irregular sloping surface of Nancy's Pass.

The following morning without trails we climbed over Dead Horse Pass and four hours later we arrived at Minaret Lake at 9,793 feet. We found obsidian chips scattered along this cross-country route. Our campsite was set up on the east shore overlooking the lake. Behind us off in the distance to the east was Nancy's Pass. By visually following her ridgeline, it dropped almost 3,000 feet into the valley below. To the west towering above us were the seventeen jagged peaks of the Minarets. Riegelhuth, Star, Michael, Davis, Lenard and Clyde (named after a few the early famous Sierra mountain climbers) just to name a few of the Minarets. The town of Independence, California, dedicated a museum to one of those climbers, Norman Clyde. The peak bearing his name at 12,261 feet was the tallest narrow peak in this mountain range.

The following morning will be a layover day for an opportunity to hike a side adventure with only our daypacks to locate and explore the historic Minaret Mines.

Five
Minaret Mine Trek
August 08, 2012

We spent the night along the east bank of Minaret Lake. The following morning we started our side trip to the historic Minaret Mine at 9,800 feet. Once again, we checked our map for a used trail following the drainage canyon north from the lake.

First we tried a high approach to avoid following the canyon as it dropped in elevation. We climbed over a hundred feet in elevation before realizing this used trail led us to a class 3 drop-off of 80 plus feet. Without the proper equipment, we had no choice but to double back down the canyon and follow the run-off stream. After a short distance, on an elevated slope to the left, was a marker. Maybe by climbing toward the marker, the saddle behind it may lead to a forgotten trail toward the mine. Once at the saddle, looking down into the valley, could that be a structure parochially hidden by a grove of trees?

After crossing a couple of dry streambeds and skirting around downed timber, directly in front of us on the hillside was an A-frame type structure. Closer review revealed that this building covered the vertical Baysore Mine Shaft. A short distance north was another mine opening with ore car rails leading from the main mine shaft. The rails crossed an earth bridge to what looked like an ore loading area.

Throughout the area were a few cabin foundations, decades

Close up view of Minaret Lake.

ago they could have been living quarters. One lonely log shed was still standing with a few old discarded tools, shovels, saws, ax handle, steel rollers and even a coffee pot hanging on its wall. Outside the entrance of this shed was the trolley of an old discarded rusted ore car. Across a small ravine was the second mine shaft with tailings scattered down the hillside.

When I returned from my ten-day adventure, my curiosity concerning the history of this out of the way mine kept nagging at me. The Minaret Mine was established in 1878 by J W Starkweather. The most profitable mineral was lead followed by silver, gold and copper. In 1881 they surveyed the area for a railroad system over Mammoth Pass but failed to get state approval. They went public and sold 150,000 shares for 10 cents each. Even with the mine's rich minerals, the labor and transportation costs drained their profits. The main shaft reached a depth of 300 feet before closure sometime in the early 1930's. Legendary dog musher, Tex Couchane, made regular supply and mail runs during the winter to keep the mine operational year around.

In 1960, Dr. Ralph York reopened the mine and invited his family and friends to have fun mining. Maybe we could call this a working resort? The Minaret Mine stayed operational until the 1990's, then it was given to the USFS. Almost all the log structures have been torn down or removed by the forest service as a safety hazard.

The National Park Service attempted to annex 30,000 acres of the Minaret Mountains into Yosemite National Park. But the mining interests during the time blocked that action. Article printed in the Los Angeles Times dated November 03, 1927.

We spent over three hours walking through part of the Minaret Mountain mining district. One day I will return not to look for gold or silver, but somewhere in those discarded tailings were larger pieces of the mineral called agate.

View of log structure and tailings from the Minaret Mine in the background.

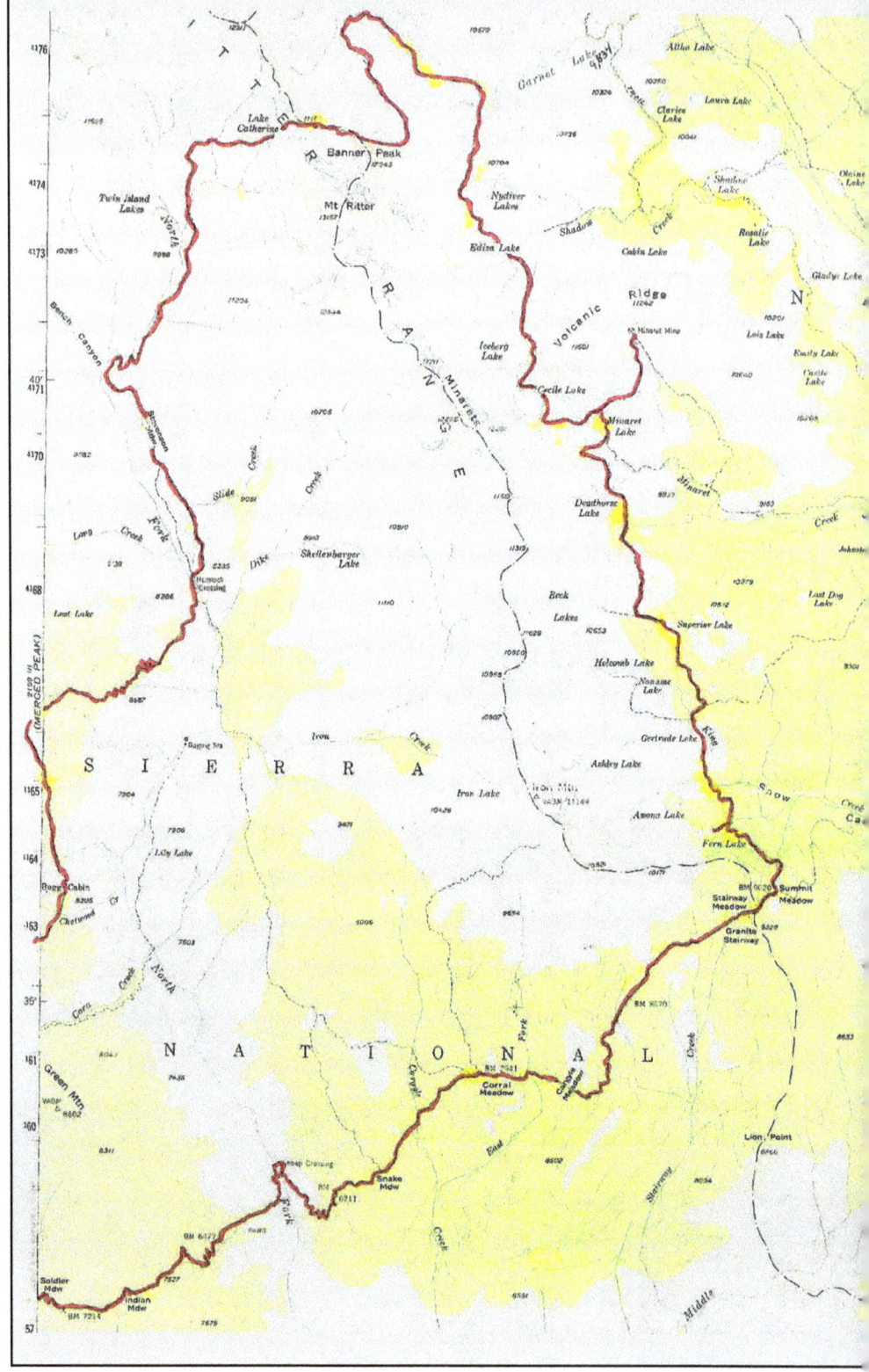

Six
Trekking through the Minarets
August 12, 2012

    The previous evening we met two mountain climbers, Mark from Chicago and Richard from Washington DC. Their goal was to climb a few Minaret peaks then complete their Sierra adventure to Tuolumne Meadows. We wished them luck; maybe we'd cross paths in the next few days.

    Around 12:30 p.m. we broke camp at Minaret Lake and continued our adventure to the north side of the Minarets. On our next mountain pass, we climbed another 500 feet into a short class three climbing area. I enjoyed these mountain saddles and was always surprised trying to anticipate the views on the opposite side. Once at the top, our focus changed to boulder hopping 500 feet down and along the north side of Cecile Lake at 10,239 feet. No trails, we just pick the friendliest boulders to skip across for the next two hours. This rocky pass was one of our difficult days, boulder hopping on both sides of the pass.

    The stress of our adventure today was forgotten when looking at the north face of these jagged mountains. The face and canyons were still covered with large patches of snow. But the steep larger canyons displayed the century old glaciers extending down to the lake surface.

Catherine Lake with Ritter and Banner Peaks in the background.

Once we arrived at the outlet of Cecile Lake, looking down another 500 feet was Iceberg Lake at 9,774 feet. We started dropping to this picturesque mountain lake using the same technique descending Cecile Lake. Our campsite that evening was located along its northern outlet. I found a huge boulder to block the gusting cold evening wind sweeping over the lakes surface to set up my tent.

The following morning we climbed over White Bark Pass at 10,500 feet. Our objective was to set up camp at Thousand Island Lake at 9,840 feet. We encountered almost three miles of variable terrain before arriving at the first of two valleys. We passed White Bark Lake and Idiza Lake before climbing another few hundred feet over the next saddle and drop to Garnett Lake. Then we started climbing again until reaching the saddle overlooking the valley at the east end of Thousand Island Lake. This huge lake was over two miles in length with many small islands. Its strange geographic name was visual while descending from the pass. That evening penetrating its darkened northern shore was the light of many campsites. The John Muir Trail crossed the northern boundary of Thousand Island Lake, which made this location ideal for overnight camping.

The following morning we climbed over the highest pass, Glacier Lake Pass at 11,158 feet. Next we passed Lake Catherine at 11,070 feet, a typical high elevation lake without trees, just rocks surrounding its surface. Then it was time to follow the northern shoreline to its outlet before starting our descent. The outlet from Catherine Lake was one of the main tributaries of the North Fork of the San Joaquin River. Mount Ritter at 13,157 feet and Mount Banner at 12,945 feet were the two highest peaks in the Minaret Range located on the southern border of Catherine Lake.

As we were descending following the major run-off stream, someone yelled, "Hello! Remember us?" It was Mark and Richard, the mountain climbers we met earlier. They camped out on the only flat spot on the canyon wall. They had just climbed Mount Davis, so the five of us took a short break to catch up on our previous three days. It's great to see someone you know within the isolated mountain wilderness.

I must confess, it was a rough afternoon descending through and around the canyon stream. At two separate areas we used ropes to lower our packs through a class 3 steep area. Finally at 10,000 feet, we arrived at a tree covered location next to a mountain stream. Soon we realized this was an old abandoned silver or gold mining area. Tailings were visible on the canyon walls above us. Fred found a souvenir in the streambed just below the waterfall, a rock with royal blue specks within its surface. Those spots could be gold or silver!

If someone was mining in the area, there must have been a trail for hauling out their ore. We found the used trail, but time and landslides offered a resistance as we followed this path that dropped 500 feet in under a quarter of a mile into the canyon below.

At one point we had to wade across this stream. No boulders to practice our balancing to the opposite side. Without my boots I realized I'm still a tenderfoot. Even the waterfalls grew in size as each tributary entered this main stream.

Descending to Iceberg Lake along cross-country route through the Minaret Mountain Range.

Our final night was spent at Hemlock Crossing at 7,560 feet. Along the trail before entering the camping, area a 15-foot waterfall greeted us. I did have the nerve to tolerate the cold mountain water that evening. Yes, it was cold, but being clean again was worth the challenge.

The following morning we hiked 10 miles, 450 feet of elevation gain and a descent of almost 500 feet before reaching the trailhead at Isberg Pass. After nine days, hundreds of feet of elevation gain and an equal amount of descending, we completed our 47-mile adventure following the words and wisdom put to pen in Steve Roper's book, Sierra High Route.

Seven
Snaffle Bit Trail
October 11, 2015

What is a snaffle bit? Are you confused? Well, I was until this proper name was explained. A snaffle bit is used to control a horse by inserting the bit in its mouth. The name snaffle is a German title for which the bit was named. Now let me tell you how this ancient trail got its name; Snaffle Bit Trail.

The Snaffle Bit Trail originated during the 1890's and was primarily used by the US Army Calvary during the early years of Yosemite National Park. Of course, the local packers, and a few hikers were looking for a route to fish Crescent, Johnson, Grouse, and Royal Arch Lakes, this trail was the only route.

According to Mrs. Anita Fulmer, the local historian who's family dates back to the first settlers in our area, she and her husband, Malcolm, rode horses along this trail many times since the 1930's. She stated they were in their 80's the last time they tried to complete the trail and sad to say it was impassable on horseback. Not only was the trail overgrown with Bear Clover, the numerous fallen trees across the trail made it impossible for their horses to continue. After 35 years with lack of usage and trail maintenance, the historic trail was returning back to nature.

After my conversation with Mrs. Fulmer I decided to put my skills to the test and see if I could locate and follow this forgotten trail. My first setback was that our recent maps don't show this historic

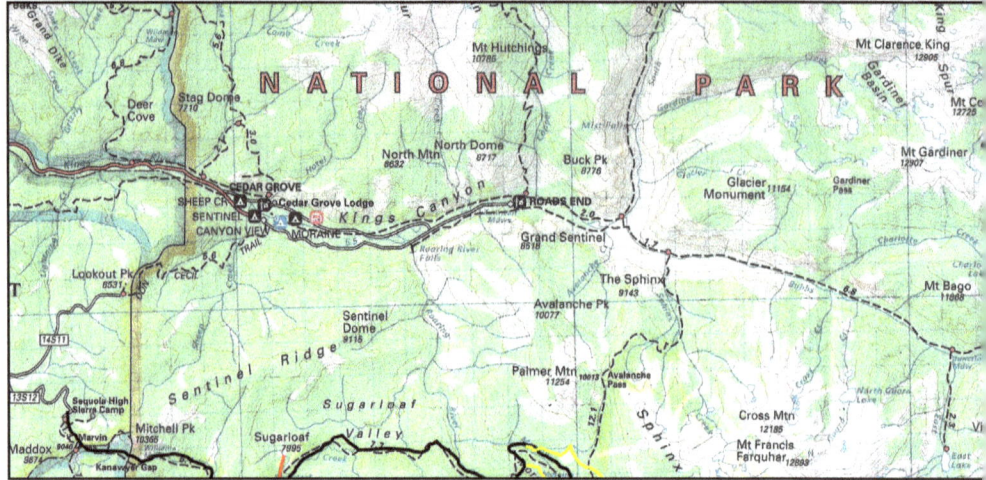

route. Luckily, I had a Yosemite map dated 1909, and it showed an unnamed broken line from Wawona to the Crescent Lake area. The only way to find out if this was the trail was to plan a hike. The trail started in Wawona just north of the swinging bridge that crossed the South Fork of the Merced River.

First I drove past the Wawona Hotel, crossed over the Merced River Bridge to the Chilnualna Road, which leads to the village of Wawona. I drove over the Chilnualna Creek and followed to the end of road, which was the trailhead to the Swinging Bridge. Once arriving at the swinging bridge the trail to the left (north) was the path starting the Snaffle Bit Trail.

Only 200 yards into my hike and to my surprise hanging from a pine tree was a red flag streaming in the breeze. Could it be possible someone has marked (flagged) this forgotten trail? Even though the trail was overgrown in places with Bear Clover and Manzanita Bushes, fallen trees tested my crawling and climbing skills. I was thankful to the individual who took the time hanging the red flags, which helped me negotiate this historic trail.

I limited myself to three hours of hiking time. At that point, I would start my return back to the swinging bridge. Part of my time was looking around the trunk of the older trees for any verification of the telephone line from Wawona to Buck Camp. Supposedly the cable was constructed in the early 1900's. You guessed it, time has removed all traces of that cable. Checking my watch, I only had 15 minutes

Swinging Bridge on Merced River at the Snaffle Bit Trailhead.

A portion of the Snaffle Bit Trail which hasn't been maintained for over five decades.

remaining to locate the end of this five-mile trail. My map revealed I'd crossed six streams, four of them dry. Estimating that I'd hiked a distance of only four miles, I had face the possibility that I might have to return without the photograph of the Snaffle Bit Blaze embedded in an elderly Cedar Tree.

The story associated with this imprint started sometime around 1900 when an Army Calvary patrol was on maneuvers. One of the horses broke its leg and was out of commission. They removed all the equipment from the horse, and the bit was attached to a tree to identify the location of the discarded gear. The bit was left attached to a tree. Who knows how long it remained at that location before someone removed it, but the impression of the bit remained as a permanent scar. My goal was to locate the tree and take a photo of the impression.

While searching for the tree, I ran out of time. I planned to return and see if that tree was still standing so I could take its photo.

Eight
Return to the Snaffle Bit Trail
October 29, 2015

I had vowed to return to the Snaffle Bit Trail and continue my quest to locate the imprint of a snaffle bit embedded on a cedar tree. Once again I stood at the trailhead, but this time, I shared the adventure with my two hiking buddies, Clem Bingham and Fred Cochran.

We welcomed the sight of our first seasonal rain the previous day; this could change the trail conditions. Hiking this trail the previous week with the knee-high bear clover leaves absent of moisture was only a memory. Sharing this dampness were the Manzanita bushes that were extending in places over the trail seven feet. We were soaked from the knees down, and our jackets shared the same fate. Even with this natural obstacle to overcome we continued to search for the Cedar Tree with the impression of a horse bit.

We added a GPS to our list of hiking supplies and maybe this instrument would help solve the mystery. My personal map dated 1909 of the Yosemite and Wawona area showed a trail leading off the Snaffle Bit trail called the Crescent Lake or Archie Leonard Trail. Now we had two separate mysteries to solve during the day's outing.

Finally after 3.6 miles, we arrived at a campsite overlooking the South Fork of the Merced River. Could this be the end of trail? From our previous research, this trail should be around five miles in length. But at this point, we hiked only 3.6 miles. We circled this area forging our way through thick underbrush and steep slopes but could

Old Snaffle Bit Trail skirting next to a cliff.

not locate a continuation of this forgotten trail. Maybe we were given the incorrect mileage figures?

I must state that after five hours of hiking and walking around over 30 cedar trees along this forgotten trail, there was no trace of the Snaffle Bit Blaze. Also the junction of the Crescent or Archie Leonard Trail was still a mystery.

On November 14, 2015, I started my third adventure following this historic trail trying to solve its two mysteries. This time, Nancy Morgan accompanied me. During the past two weeks, I communicated with Bill Wagers, the individual who placed the flags along the trail. He sent me the coordinates of the cedar tree, and he gave me the verbal location of the junction point to the Crescent or Leonard Trail.

From the location of the swinging bridge, we hiked almost two miles before the first stream. Before arriving at this canyon, on the left I noticed an open flat area that extended above the stream. From Mr. Wager's verbal information, this could be the start of the Crescent Trail. We followed this pathway over a half hour as it maneuvered up the mountain. We took a GPS reading before returning back to the Snaffle Bit Trail. With days becoming shorter that time of year, I decided I'd return in the spring of 2016 hopefully to complete the trail to where it intersects the Chilnualna Trail at higher elevation.

Time slipped by quickly while searching for an unknown within the wilderness. We hiked over another mile climbing over downed trees and looking for those pink ribbons to stay on the trail. We realized with our late start that morning, daylight would be a problem to continue beyond the camp above the river. We didn't find the Cedar Tree with the blaze, but the junction to the Crescent and Leonard Trail was no longer a mystery.

The winter snows were almost upon us, and I'd have to wait until the following year to solve this mystery. Maybe if the weather settled down, I'd have a window of opportunity in the next few days to attempt another hike. Snaffle Bit Blaze where are you?

Nine
Snaffle Bit Tree, where are you?
November 23, 2015

After three attempts to locate that historic Cedar Tree standing somewhere along the five miles of the Snaffle Bit Trail, I decided a fourth attempt was necessary. Checking with the weather station, they stated that the next day could be a possibility for a hike at 5,000 feet. After communicating with Fred Cochran, and if we wanted to solve this mystery in 2015, we should start our search the following morning.

Even with the possibility of rain and snow forecasted for the next evening, we departed from the trailhead at Wawona at 7:00 AM. The temperature was just above freezing and that layer of ice on the surface of the swinging bridge that crossed the Merced River verified that snow could be in the evenings forecast. I was relieved that the Bear Clover and Manzanita Bushes have been shedding their moisture from the first snow a few days before. At least my jacket and pants would be dry for the adventure.

The trail hadn't changed since my previous hike. The Bear Clover was still knee-high, and those many snags or fallen trees across the forgotten trail tested our climbing skills once again. After the first mile, we checked out the possible junction of the Crescent Trail, which was abandoned some 60 years ago. That was another mystery

Tony pointing to the impression of a snaffle bit embedded into an ancient Cedar Tree along the trail.

associated with this trail that will not be solved until next year because of time. Those seasonal streams that were almost dry from our four-year drought were showing signs of life. Once again, I want to thank Bill Wagers for flagging this abandoned trail back in 2007.

    After three hours following this trail, we realized our mistake in trail finding. Roughly 50 yards before arriving at the area that we thought last week was the end of the trail. Three separate flags were hanging from a Pine Tree next to a ravine. After a closer inspection, there was a trail following down into the ravine. At the bottom it crossed a small stream. On the opposite side, hanging on another pine tree was another flag. We followed the trail downstream a short distance before continuing north toward the Merced River. If this was the correct trail, within a half-mile, we would see the old Cedar Tree with the blaze of the historic Snaffle Bit embedded on its trunk.

    Luck was smiling on us. Less than 30 minutes on the north side of the trail was a huge Cedar Tree displaying the blaze of a horse bit. We put to rest the myth and identified the path as the Snaffle Bit

Fred pointing upstream from the Old Army Campsite.

Trail. This impression was located on the west side of the tree facing the trail. Only 30 yards beyond the blaze-covered tree was the largest Sugar Pine Tree I've ever seen. This ancient tree had a girth of eight plus feet and stood over 120 feet high. If you decide to visit these historic sentinels next year, remember if you see the Sugar Pine Tree first, double back 30 yards to the blaze on the large Cedar Tree.

We continued following this trail another quarter-mile until reaching the North Fork of the Merced River. There was a campsite above the river, and this was the location of trail's end. I wonder how many times the US Calvary used this campsite after the trail originated in 1896?

The Snaffle Bit Trail does exist, but if you decide to witness this tree first hand you'll have to wait for the snow melts in the spring.

Ten
Treasures of Death Valley
March 24, 2014

    This was my fourth consecutive year for another exciting adventure into the desert and mountains of Death Valley. The last week in March and the first two weeks in April were the ideal times to visit this colorful place of nature. Temperatures on the valley floor during the night were around 48 degrees and during the day 78 to 92 degrees. If one waits until after May first, daytime temperatures can exceed 107 degrees.

    After driving past Stovepipe Wells, the distant mounds of the Mesquite Sand Dunes come into view. The shadows from the evening sun gave these dunes a different personality. They were a must see both early morning (sunrise) and late evening (sunset) for that unique photo opportunity.

    The drive west on the road toward Scotty's Castle kept us excited just looking at the multicolored mountains lining the highway. On previous trips, this historic castle was on my vacation schedule. Nancy and I set up our first campsite at Mesquite Springs Campground. This picturesque campground was located next to the main Death Valley Wash before Scotty's Castle.

    The following day we drove past Ubehebe Crater, which challenged us to hike around its two-mile perimeter last year. The smaller of the two craters was located directly behind it. Interesting

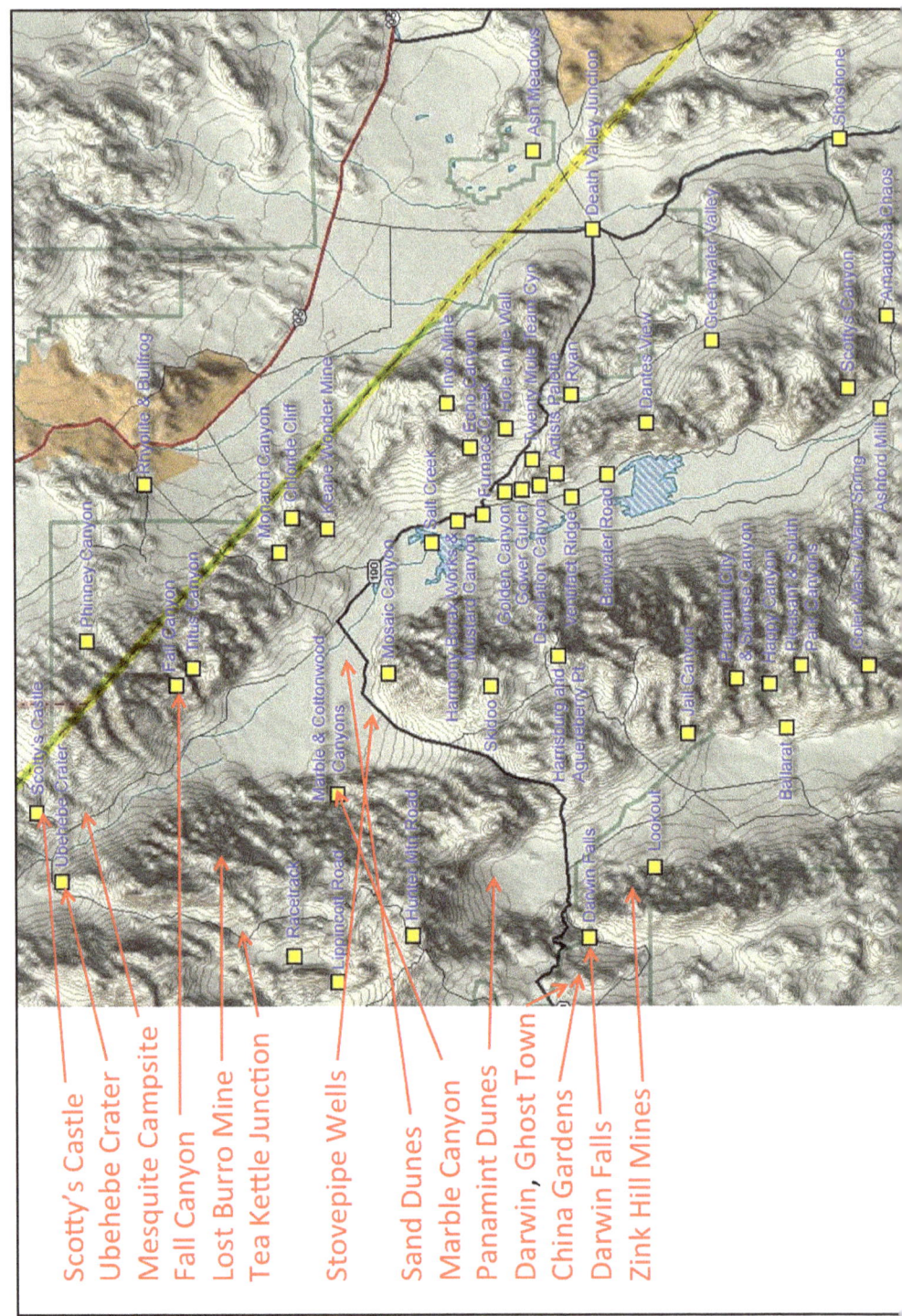

Mountain Secrets Revealed

how the sand surrounding the entire area was black from the intense heat created thousands of years ago. We faced 20 plus miles on the sand and rock desert road (Race Track Road) to Tea Kettle Junction. Yes, Tea Kettle Junction! This was a lonesome road sign constructed in the middle of the desert. Hanging from this triangular shape sign were teakettles of all shapes and sizes placed and signed by passing tourists.

The desert road followed between the Cottonwood Mountain Range and Last Chance Range. Normally, the desert floor was covered with wildflowers, but I believed we were two weeks too early this trip. The Barrel and Beaver Tail Cactus along with the Joshua Trees have started to bloom. Maybe when we return in six days, we'll be rewarded with new desert colors.

At Tea Kettle Junction we followed the Hidden Valley Road to the Lost Burrow Mine junction. Then followed another one-lane

Ubehebe crater over a mile in diameter. Created millions of years ago wile the earth was cooling. Trail circles perimeter of crater.

Death Valley's Lost Burro Mine with active claims today.

desert 4x4 road climbing in elevation to the mine. We were less than a quarter of a mile from the mine when this mining road became unsafe to drive. After a short hike, I had my first view of the miner's cabin and discarded cabin foundations. On the adjacent mountainside was a huge wooden loading structure. On the opposite side were the tailings from eleven working mines. This mine was discovered in April 1907 by Bert Shively, an active prospector in Death Valley. Gold and Silver were its principal minerals.

A small canyon separated the main mines from the mill. Following the canyon in elevation to the ridge surprised me. From that location I stared down into the valley 1,900 feet looking at the road that we drove on earlier in the morning. Along the road was the enormous historic dry lakebed called the Race Tract. It was noted for stones that mysteriously moved across the dry lakebed and leaving trails. After almost four hours of adventure, it was time to hike back down to my vehicle and back to the road junction.

Our next destination was called Rest Springs. We followed another desert 4x4 road ten miles to 6,500 feet. At this point, we started hiking to Rest Springs and continued in elevation to Burro Springs

Tea Kettle Junction at the cross roads to Lost Burro Mine and the famous Race Track. Only 26 miles from a paved road.

around 7,200 feet. History states that in the year 1917, a pipeline was constructed from Burro Springs down to the valley and up to Lost Burrow Mine. This gave the miners the option of processing the ore at the mining site. There were still sections of rusted pipe along the remote canyon. After hiking another two hours, we were running out of daylight, so Burro Springs would have to wait for another day.

We set up our tent along the canyon just below Rest Springs. The following morning our tent had accumulated ice on its outside surface. To my surprise, the morning temperature dropped below 30 degrees. We made a quick cup of hot coffee, broke camp and started the twelve plus miles back to Tea Kettle Junction.

After 4-wheeling over a two-foot shelf, which I had to build so my vehicle could continue, we faced yet another canyon on our right. Being curious I stopped my vehicle and started walking into its shadows. This isolated box canyon was sheltering numerous fossils embedded into the larger boulders and walls. Death Valley sure had surprises! We continued our drive another four miles following this road back to Tea Kettle Junction.

Race Track is a dry lakebed. Stones move across its surface during the night creating grooved trails.

We drove another few miles to the Race Track and looked for the moving stones. The National Park Service told me that nighttime temperatures dropping below freezing conditions caused the tracks. If during that time the wind picked up to extreme speeds, the rocks would blow across the sand and leave tracks. After walking on the dry lakebed surface photographing those mysterious tracks, it was back to my vehicle. I proceeded to the dry campground at the base of the Lippincott Mine area.

Eleven
Treasures of Death Valley
March 27, 2014

The dry camping area below the Lippincott Mines was at 4,000 feet. All I could see surrounding me was sagebrush, cactus, rock, and sand. The dry camp had only designated parking spaces with no trees, restrooms or water.

After researching the Death Valley map, there were two old roads, upper and lower to the Lippincott Mines. First, I attempted driving my Jeep following the abandoned desert road through a dry streambed, only to realize my vehicle was lacking enough ground clearance, and I almost got stuck! The original road, over time, washed away all the small rocks that filled in those natural spaces between larger rocks. Maybe larger diameter tires would have solved this problem. I turned around and drove back to the campsite. If we wanted to preview the Lippincott Mines we'd have to refer back to our original mode of travel; hiking.

The minerals of copper, lead, silver, and zinc were the primary materials extracted from the Lippincott Mines. The earliest mining activity around the area was in December 1906. There was a common ownership between each of the mines. Raven Mine, Lead King Mine, and Southern Lead Mine all had unknown production until 1942. That was the time George Lippincott first leased and then purchased the property for development. They even used the dry lakebed

Lippencott Mine. principal ore was lead followed by silver and zinc.

(Race Track) as a landing field for business purposes. These were very rich mines with 65% lead and 35 ounces of silver per ton. Up until 1954 they produced 2,000 tons of lead, silver, and zinc. It was still the third largest producer of lead in Death Valley. History states that before 1942 over 2,000 feet of shafts were hidden within the mines.

Surprising the amount of discarded history still remaining in this area, like abandoned foundations and a huge water tank converted from a semi-trailer. Almost hidden on the hillside was the chassis of a discarded truck, which still had its wooden spoke wheels intact. Many items such as storage bins, railroad ties, and material loaders all made from wooden planks. Rusted cables used to transport material in buckets were still clinging to the mountain side.

Rather than walk back to the main area along the upper road, we decided to descend down the mountain and create our own route to the lower road. One questionable area through a narrow canyon slot, hand holds were necessary for stability. This maneuver saved over an hour of hiking in this desert heat.

Death Valley Main Wash. leading to the remote channels containing fossils.

The lower road led to another huge mine entrance with its adjoining wooden loading structure and storage bin. I must confess, I explored the insides of a few of the mines. But I used caution and limited myself to those mines with reinforced beams or tunneling through hard rock. Another attraction created from the tailings removed from these mines was the shelves that gave us a platform for viewing the distant canyons and mountains.

Late afternoon, unknown to us, a desert sandstorm was brewing at the west end of the valley. I noticed this brown cloud when gazing toward the distant mountains. Could this be a sandstorm? Ten minutes later we were surrounded by high winds and sand blowing through our campsite. We sought shelter within my vehicle before the winds arrived. Lucky I blocked our tent with my jeep, and that kept it from blowing to the far corners of the desert. The storm only lasted 10 minutes, but now we have sand inside of everything. I had to shake out my sleeping bag before nightfall.

After two days of adventure exploring around this remote campground, the time came to break camp and continue the 26-mile drive back to Mesquite Campground. I just wanted to make a personal comment concerning the corduroy type road. If your vehicle had no rattles, it did now! If you had a few loose parts on your vehicle's suspension, don't worry they're not there now, because they fell off!

While we were setting up our new campsite at Mesquite Campground, we were approached by Jay and Liz, who were seasoned Death Valley hikers. That evening they suggested two separate hiking adventures within a three-mile radius of our campground.

The following morning we hiked across the Death Valley Wash, located a gentle slope on the western canyon side and climbed its steep wall. We started our hike across the plateau toward the Cottonwood Mountain Range. Our objective was to locate the petroglyphs concealed somewhere inside one of the canyons. When we returned six hours later, our only comment was, "We'll be back next year and search again!"

The morning of our last full day, I looked forward to the new six-mile round trip hike. We hiked west up the same wash and located another canyon. Jay and Liz stated that one canyon might have fossils dating back 10,000 years when Death Valley was a huge lake. Before noon we located three separate natural springs and all displayed footprints of the local inhabitants. We crossed the huge Death Valley Wash and located the remote canyon that Jay and Liz had spoken about. The wash would lead us to the base of the Cottonwood Mountain Range. Our final day turned out to be a success because we found fossils embedded within the canyon walls.

On our return, we stopped at the largest of the three natural springs we passed earlier in the morning. We found obsidian chips and even a small piece of flint, which the American Indians used centuries ago for fire starting.

Overall this was a successful six days hiking these remote canyons and mountains of Death Valley. The only disappointment of this adventure was a dry season and no wildflowers to photograph.

Twelve
Death Valley's Darwin Falls
April 07, 2015

Once again I took the time to challenge that mystical place called Death Valley. I decided to delay my vacation two weeks hoping to avoid the high winds that accompany the last spring season. I almost succeeded. The first two days Nancy and I were confined to the comforts of the tent cabin we rented at Panamint Springs. The reason for staying at Panamint Springs was to be close to Darwin Falls.

The following morning, winds were still blowing at high speeds across the desert. We decided to take a chance and drive to the trailhead leading toward Darwin Falls, which was located inside of steep canyon walls. The 2.5 miles of a sand and rock road was much gentler than expected. A passenger car with average ground clearance could maneuver over the road. At the trailhead, the surrounding mountains blocked the nasty winds as we started our hike into the narrow but colorful canyon. Native plants, rabbit brush and indigo brush grew along the narrow wash. Following the narrow stream into the canyon, the vegetation changed to thickets of willows, tamarisk, cattail, and rushes.

The deep narrows of Darwin Canyon were among the lushest and beautiful in the park. This short walk to the lower waterfall was a wonderful illustration of the miracle of water in the desert. We hiked only 15 minutes into the canyon before walking the area where this stream appeared on the canyon floor. As we hiked further into the

Zinc Hill Mines. located four miles on a 4x4 road from the trailhead to Darwin Falls. One top of the mountain above the Falls.

China Gardens. located three miles below the Zinc Hill Mines. A natural spring supports these 100 year old Coy Fish. This was a processing area to separate the ore, zinc, silver, gold, led and copper. Principal ore was zinc.

Ghost Town of Darwin. abandoned in the 1950's. Darwin processed ore removed from the neighboring mountain mines.

remote canyon, the welcome sight of small ponds enticed our curiosity to forge on toward the falls. Another 20 minutes and we were standing at the base of Darwin Falls, 18 feet high, surrounded by trees and lush vegetation.

History states that the old dirt road was part of the original Toll Road built by Bob Eichbaum that led to Stovepipe Wells. The area was first visited by Dr. Darwin French, who established a base camp when he led his first prospecting expedition into Death Valley in the 1850's.

Just before entering the lower parking area and trailhead there was a directional fork in the road. We continued to the left of the parking area where a 4-wheel drive vehicle was recommended. We followed this road for 3.9 winding miles up past Zinc Hill Mines. All that remained was a huge wooden material loader and a circular well-shaped pit that separated the ore before it entered the loader. Once past the mines, this desert road drops down another 1.1 miles to another junction. We followed this sandy road to the right another 3.5 miles which led to China Garden Spring. This was the processing location for the Zinc Ore from the mines. All that remained were rock walls, metal and wood structures which were processing and loading buildings. Trees and vegetation surrounded a natural spring. It looked like an oasis hidden in this remote canyon in the middle of the desert. We were in for a surprise when entering this green area surrounding this natural spring. The pond was inhabited by goldfish or koi fish. The name China Garden made sense.

I doubled back to the fork and continued driving on the opposite dirt road to Miller Springs. These springs were abandoned when the Zinc Mining was closed in the early part of the 20th century. Only three structures remain, with one containing the ancient pumping machinery. We continued following this same road to the small abandoned mining town of Darwin, established in 1874. During its prosperous times, this mining town boasted over 2,000 people. When the mining era came to a close, most of its population departed for other active mining towns. Its population was only 50 persons on our visit. We only found one stop sign at the town's main crossroads. This road led to a paved road that ends at Highway 190 and back to Panamint Springs Resort.

When we arrived back to Panamint Springs, the wind was still blowing around our tent cabin. We'd have to cook inside again, otherwise the wind would blow our stove and dishes off the picnic table. We hoped the wind would die down by morning before we started our second adventure hiking across the desert to the Panamint Dunes.

Darwin Falls, located one mile north of Panamint Springs, two miles off of highway 190 and follow up with a four mile round-trip hike.

Thirteen
Death Valley's Panamint Dunes
April 08, 2015

After two evenings of high winds, we welcomed a calm morning with only a slight breeze. We packed up our vehicle, departed to the desert floor and located the lonely desert road that led to the trailhead for Panamint Dunes. They were located on the north end of Panamint Valley at the foot of Hunter Mountain. Five miles east of Panamint Springs on Highway 190, we located the dirt road called Big Four Mine Road leading to the trailhead. Only a high clearance vehicle was needed on these 4.9 miles of desert road. There were a few washouts and ruts as was common on the desert surface.

Ten minutes into the drive we came across the first artifacts. They were quite large and boasted a brownish rust color. There were two rusted, abandoned vehicles just off the road. After close inspection, one was a 1941 Buick 2 door sedan and the second was a 1955 Buick Roadmaster 4 door sedan. All that remained was their rusted shells. Could they be a friendly reminder that Death Valley chooses which visitor she wants to keep?

Forty minutes later we arrived at the trailhead. Off in the distance, 3.4 miles away, was our destination, Panamint Dunes. From where we stood they looked very small. This would be a true desert adventure across the sandy valley. No trail because the dunes will be in view throughout our hike. We'd have a gradual 800 feet of elevation gain and our morning temperature was perfect, hovering in the fifties.

Discarded 55 Buick and 41 Buick along road to Panamint Dunes.

Tony hiked to the top of the sand dunes.

Looking down at the desert floor, the native creatures were quite active the previous night leaving their prints. There were mostly lizard tracks, but rabbit, fox, coyote, roadrunner and a small snake scarred the smooth sandy floor. One small resident of this vast desert revealed its camouflaged position when it moved. We were rewarded with a few photos of a small Desert Horn Toad.

The most common bushes covering the sandy surface were creosote and bursage. The low gray-green bushes responsible for the spiny burs we picked off our socks were called dodder or devil's guts. Quite a few flowering spring plants added vibrant colors to the landscape. Evening primrose, desert gold, and the most colorful, the prickle poppy with its blue-green colors of spring were among the showiest.

After two hours of hiking, we arrived at the base of the distant dunes. They sure grew in size after three miles of hiking. Could it have been the backdrop of the surrounding mountains that dwarfed the rolling white sands of these mounds?

Our goal was to climb to the saddle between the south and middle dunes. We struggled through the pristine white sand for almost another half-mile and over 300 feet of elevation gain before we reached our destination. I continued to climb to the top of the center dune. Each time I struggled to a crest, there was another higher mound in the distance. It was time to sit and relax on this huge sandy cushion and enjoy the distant views of the enormous valley.

My second reward that morning came while sitting on my sandy perch. Off in the distance, an F16 Air Force Fighter Jet and its pilot were practicing their maneuvers just above the valley surface. With the sound trailing quite a distance behind his aircraft, he was difficult to spot. Now I realize why I kept coming back to Death Valley every year. Each new adventure was a challenge, but with that challenge comes reward.

Fourteen
Death Valley Fall Canyon
April 09, 2015

After completing the hike to the Panamint Dunes, we drove past Stovepipe Wells and continued to Mesquite Campground. This was our camping area for the next two days because Scotty's Castle and Fall Canyon were located close by. The terrible winds we experienced the last two days were now just a gentle desert breeze.

How can one visit Death Valley without spending time viewing the craftsmanship and history associated with Scotty's Castle only 5.6 miles from Mesquite Campground? This was my third visit and maybe I'd discover something new to photograph. Albert Johnson, the original owner and builder of the castle, completed his dream with the friendship and help of Walter Scott (Death Valley Scotty). This year I finally saw Albert Johnson's main mode of transportation as he traveled the early desert roads. It was a 1914 Packard, seven passenger, open touring, automobile. This 5,000 pound, aluminum bodied, 12-cylinder engine vehicle was now on display at Scotty's Castle in the main visitor's center building.

The morning of April 10th, we decided to complete the hike into Fall Canyon. Two years ago the extreme heat forced us to turn back, with only a half-mile to our destination, called the 18-foot Fall Canyon Dry Falls.

Scotty's Castle in Death Valley.

The trailhead was located on the left at the mouth of the Titus Canyon road. We followed the trail for 6/10 of a mile before it dropped into the wide wash of Fall Canyon. In several places, this wash squeezed through narrow passageways. The polished canyon walls soared vertically reaching up hundreds of feet and were topped by distant walls of the same. These sheer bare rocks had multiple colors of yellow, tan, dark brown, and red. As the day progressed, the reflected light from the sun accented the rock display. In the evening, the slanted rays of the sun picked up deeper shades of red as they reflected back and forth between the walls.

The first obvious landmark was the confluence within the first side canyon. This deep amphitheater was dominated by a tower and large boulders with the grandeur of a cathedral. The side canyon had a 13-foot dry fall with a shaded grotto just above it. Viewing this upper attraction was almost impossible because of its height and the slick rock surfaces. Even the back side had no physical entrance, with its impassible 20-foot fall.

About 3.4 miles into the canyon we finally arrived at the 18-foot dry fall that presumably gave this canyon its name. From the top of this polished blue rock fall, someone left a rope to assist anyone

Falls located within Fall Canyon. Natural color of falls (Blue).

Polished marble that graces the wall in Fall canyon.

who was brave enough to attempt the climb. My rock climbing skills couldn't handle this maneuver, so this was our turn-around point.

From checking the Death Valley book, there was a bypass, an alternate route by climbing to the upper fall on the south canyon wall around 300 feet down the wash before reaching the fall. After checking this route, first I would have to scale a short chimney and at the top there was a narrow trail that would lead above the fall. This bypass was the crux of this hike and was well worth the effort. Physically, I wouldn't be able to see the high point of the hike. I wasn't comfortable with the secondary route.

Even though the 18-foot fall was my turn-around point, just the polished colorful walls and the marble layers embedded into those steep vertical walls were my personal rewards. Our return was much easier descending the 1,330 feet to the trailhead.

Fifteen
Death Valley Marble Canyon
April 10, 2015

    I was pleased that we put Marble Canyon on our hiking list with its narrow washes, steep canyons, rock art, and fossils. Along the second narrows, we saw the ancient petroglyphs adorning the canyon walls that rank among the most elaborate in all of Death Valley.

    We traveled west of Stovepipe Wells on Highway 190 the 8.6 miles of desert road that led to the edge of Cottonwood Wash. From this sandy parking area, we continued with the recommended high clearance (or 4x4 vehicle). We followed the wash into the mountains another 2.2 miles to the road junction. A tall metal direction sign identified the location. The road to the right continued following the wash to Marble Canyon. My lucky passenger was treated to the rock formation, flowers, and impeccable distant views. With the responsibility of driving, I practiced the skill of maneuvering around rocks and washouts that shared the colorful but historic desert road.

    From the metal road sign to the trailhead or the first narrows into the lower Marble Canyon was only 2.6 miles. Many visitors came to Marble Canyon to see the petroglyphs. These prehistoric figures were pecked on smooth rock surfaces by the native inhabitants centuries ago. The journey from the trailhead was another mile before viewing the first few petroglyphs. To anyone who enjoyed history, this was a special place. There were beautiful figures to be found, from abstract drawings such as pregnant bighorn sheep, lizards, desert foxes, human

Petroglyphs in Marble Canyon

Marble Canyon Wash in the second narrows.

figures, and finely crafted birds. Also pecked on one canyon wall was a very faint historical inscription of the date "1849" with the initials "JB" mixed with petroglyphs. Could this have been one of the men of the ill-fated Savage-Penney Party? This group of immigrants split from the Jayhawkers and left Death Valley at the end of 1849. Twelve men were among the first to see Death Valley and only two were known to have reached the coast.

After entering the first narrows and for the next two miles we walked through a colorful corridor framed by sheer high granite walls. Sharing this corridor was an interesting side canyon with falls, thick limestone beds loaded with black chert nodules and overhangs offering welcome shade. The first narrows ended with a huge quartz monzonite chockstone wedged between the canyon walls. On the right, there was a makeshift trail that led over and around the natural blockage. Once back to the wash, this was the beginning of the second narrows.

The second narrows were the most impressive within this canyon. They gradually deepened, then opened up for a short distance, before narrowing again. The polished walls continued high above

Petroglyphs in Marble Canyon within the second narrows.

the wash and opened to a smooth contoured passage. For the next hundred feet or so we walked through a dim, cool and naked world where the light continuously changed through the day. One spot along these narrows someone had etched imprints on these smooth walls. Some of these etchings were the works of modern day, would-be artists. They tried to duplicate the original petroglyphs.

After four tenths of a mile the second narrows ended and the wash opened up to an impressive extended open canyon. On the left perched on an elevated sandbar was an ideal campsite location. We set up our camp and with the few remaining hours of daylight we continued exploring the main wash. The third narrows was another 2.4 miles following this same wash. Knowing we lacked daylight to complete this round-trip, we decided to slow our progress and search the smooth rocks for petroglyphs along the canyon walls. Luck was hiking with us that evening, and our camera's captured two separate historical petroglyph sites on both sides of the wash.

The following morning we decided to hike past the images we found the previous evening and ignore the distant second narrows.

Last evening, while researching my Death Valley Book, it stated that after only a quarter mile, a large canyon to the north contained fossils. Only 15 minutes of hiking this large wash and to our right was this large canyon. As we hiked, the canyon walls became steeper with a few smaller intersecting dry side channels. Even the walls had scars from those turbulent spring run-offs.

Once again luck was following us, because within this northern canyon, fossils were embedded in the rocks. Mostly fragments of crinoids and gastropods fossils located on the polished slanted walls of dark dolomite rock. There were a few fossils embedded in large rocks lying on the canyon floor.

With the sun overhead starting its downward cycle, it was time to return to our campsite. We'd have time to break camp and return to the trailhead before the sun set in the west. It was around five o'clock when we arrived at the trailhead. I thought to myself if I could have carried an additional supply of water we could have spent another night. The weather was perfect and the afternoon temperature was around 80 degrees. Nighttime temperature only dipped down to 48 degrees.

During the two days we spent within this canyon, we only saw two hikers, and that was during the first day. They were doing a fast round trip day hike to the end of the second narrows.

Sixteen
Forgotten Wawona Stagecoach Road
October 17, 2013

During the fall of 2012 in Yosemite National Park, I first experienced the old Wawona Stagecoach Road above the Wawona Tunnel. At Vista Point, which was the beginning of the Pohono Trail, I started my short three-hour hike to the new Inspiration Point. This old Indian trail gave me my first introduction to the Old Wawona Stagecoach Road. At one point along the trail, these two historical paths crossed. In the past, I've crossed many logging roads in the wilderness, and I accepted this crossing as one of those. Once entering the Inspiration Point area, I crossed a paved road. This odd discovery activated my curiosity into researching this old forgotten road.

The following week I stopped by the local library and started researching each historic book relating to our early Yosemite Roads. How little did I know? Over time I became hooked on this historic road carved into the mountains south of Yosemite Valley. When my research revealed this 17-mile road extended from Wawona to the Yosemite Valley, I was hooked! This could be a great hike that would also update historical information.

It took over four separate trips to complete this historic journey into the past. Each segment revealed the remarkable achievements of these pioneers using picks, shovels, black power, and sweat to achieve

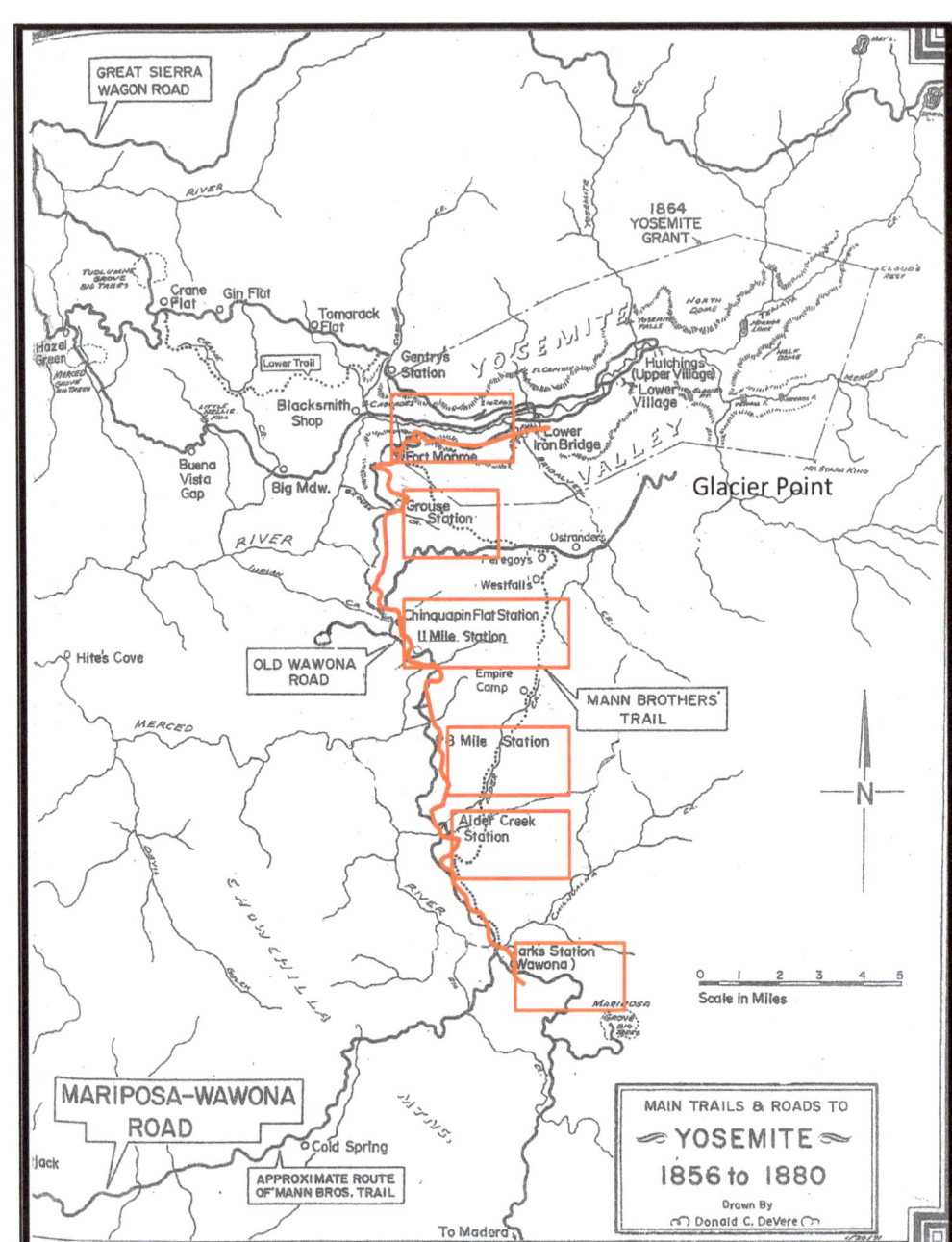

The horse and stagecoach was replaced by the horseless carriage (motorized busses). Image circa 1915, public domain.

their goals. Their only monetary reward was a wage of forty dollars a month, which included food and lodging.

The old road officially started at the covered bridge in Wawona. Then it turned west to follow the new and present Wawona Road until reaching a large flat area east of the Merced River, or just before entering the Wawona Campground. At this point, the historic road started its journey east, upward into the mountains. As I hiked this lofty road, the skills displayed by the workers surrounded me. History stated that five Italian skilled rock wall masons with experiences from their homeland created the wedge-shaped stones that supported the hand laid rock retaining walls and bridges. I found evidence of black power blasting that helped carve this untouched mountain creating the rock shelves needed for the road's flat surface.

Just over one hour into this first segment a landslide that happened decades ago removed part of the road. I had a choice to climb over or drop down to bypass this obstacle. I chose the higher route which I felt was less of a risk maneuvering around the slide area.

The number of deer scattered throughout the area surprised me. If it weren't for the noise from their trekking through the thick undergrowth, I would have missed their graceful maneuvering through the forest.

After a few miles, the road intersected with the present Wawona Road at Mosquito Creek. I followed the new road only a short distance

Abandoned Old Wawona Stagecoach Road. 1876 to 1933.

Old and New Wawona Stagecoach Road (highway #41).

Alder Creek, old bridge location on The Old Wawona Stagecoach Road.

of 50 plus yards before dropping down to the west toward Alder Creek and the Alder Creek Station. This station was removed around 1933 when the old road was closed. The bridge that crossed the creek has fallen victim to wet seasons and age. All that remained was the stone foundation and a few support logs.

The old road crossed the new Wawona Road four times before arriving at the Eight Mile Station at Bishop Creek. At this point, we followed the new road until the old road separated and departed to the west. A manmade sign placed at this section of this old road identified it as a firebreak for the Yosemite West Subdivision. The road dropped in elevation until it crossed Strawberry Creek and Eleven Mile Creek. The Eleven Mile Station was located next to this water source identified by a large flat area. The structures at the Eight and Eleven Mile Stations had been removed, and all that remained were a few rusted artifacts.

As the road continued north, it intersected with the Yosemite West Road. We hiked east back to the new Wawona Road as it followed to the Chinquapin Flat Station. Its location was next to Indian Creek, close to the point it flowed under the Wawona Road. This station

Clem along the Old Wawona Stagecoach Road, The Eleven Mile Station location.

building was also removed, but at this point, our 1890 map revealed that the old and new Wawona Road overlapped each other passing Glacier Point Road. It continued another four miles until arriving at Grouse Creek and the location of the Grouse Creek Station. Its structure was also removed decades ago.

At this point, we departed to the east from the new road and continued on the stagecoach road as it rose in elevation through the area burnt from a lightning strike during the 1990's. Even though this area of historic road was paved with asphalt, over the years the thick mountain brush had overtaken its surface, and it became difficult to forge through. The thick undergrowth was caused by natural springs flowing across the road surface. The 80 years of growth was not the resistance we expected while forging and climbing following this old mountain road. Hidden from view was this six-foot natural rectangular shaped watering hole almost twenty inches deep. Surrounding this hidden spring were the footprints of the local residents.

As this historic road climbed higher in elevation, to the west Big Meadow came into view. At the lower elevation, the new Wawona Road skirted around its northern boundary. At almost 5700 feet in elevation, the road started its descent into Yosemite Valley. Looking to the west through the trees, directly below was Turtleback Dome. Only a few hundred yards separated the dome from this road.

At the elevation around 5600 feet, we arrived at Fort Monroe. These structures were removed after the Wawona Tunnel was completed in July of 1933. All that remained was the scar of a cabin foundation and a trash dump. There was a trail located behind the area that led to the Old Inspiration Point. Passengers had the option during their layover period to hike this trail to the point and enjoy the specular views of Yosemite Valley. Fort Monroe at one time was the south entrance into Yosemite Valley.

Fort Monroe was named after stagecoach driver George H. Monroe. He drove wagons for the A. Henry Washburn Stagecoach Line in the 1880's. His reputation was flawless, and professionally he was known as the best wagon operator of that stagecoach line. We continued following the road as it dropped in elevation to the new Inspiration Point.

History stated that in the year 1876, a short distance of this road was called The Washburn Slide. Named after Henry Washburn, who was Galen Clark's partner constructing this unique road. Once the coach entered this 12% steep grade, it forced the stagecoach driver to ask the passengers to step out of the coach. They would walk for roughly 100 yards while the driver and helper disassembled the coach and carried it down the road before reassembling. The passengers seemed to enjoy this novelty before continuing their ride to the valley floor next to the Bridalveil Fall area.

Fred Cochran, Clem Bingham, and I spent four days of trial and error and finally completed another one of the forgotten trails or roadways from Yosemite's colorful history.

As a footnote, I would like to acknowledge the dreams of Galen Clark (1814-1910) the first Guardian of Yosemite National Park. Also, I acknowledge his partner Albert Henry Washburn (1836-1902) owner of the Yosemite Stage and Turnpike Company. Together, they had the foresight to construct this wilderness road from the south into Yosemite National Park back in 1876.

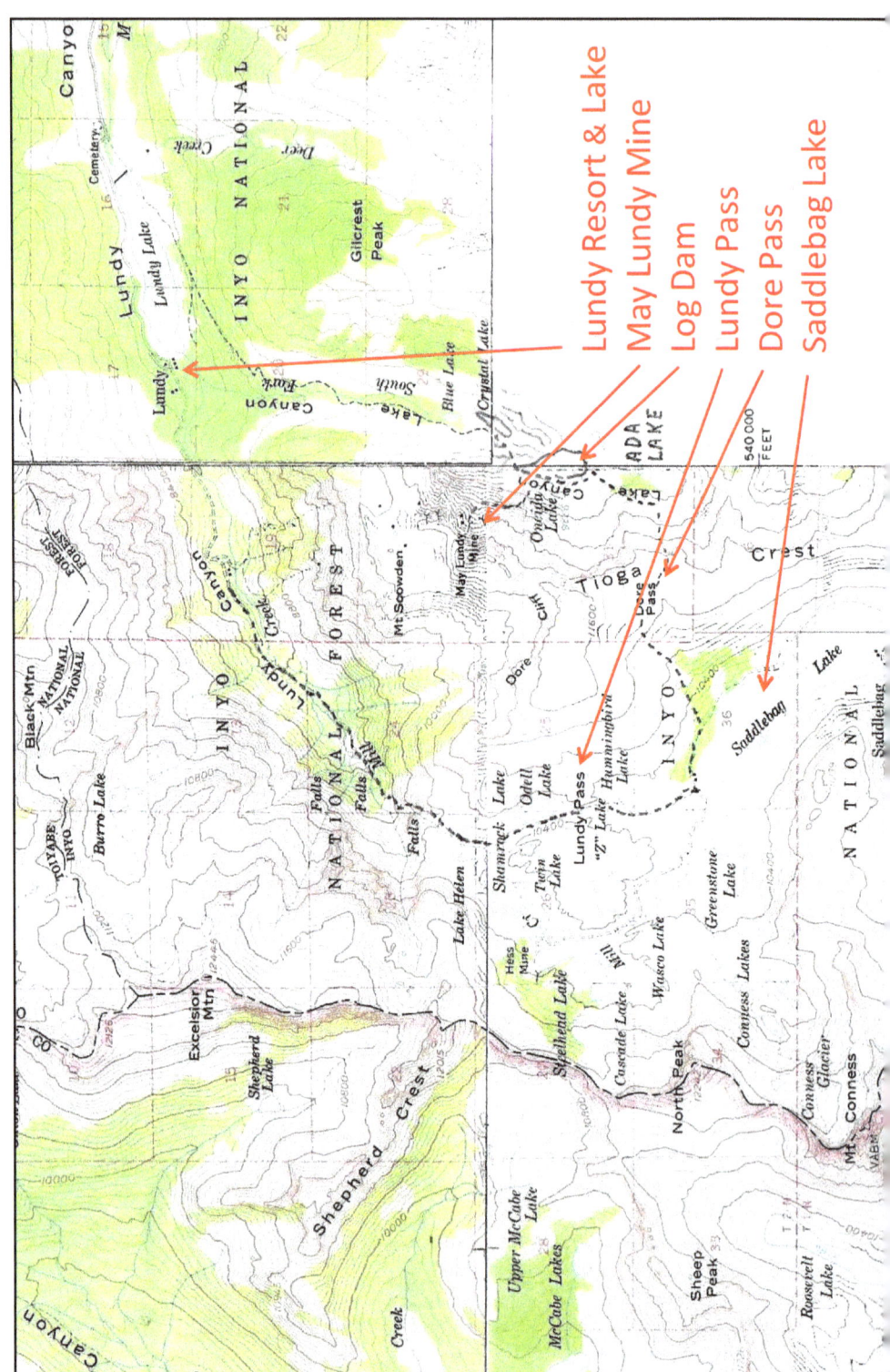

Seventeen
Lundy Canyon Mining History
July 13, 2013

Once again I decided to explore another hiking area on the east side of our Sierra Nevada Mountains? Only seven miles north from Lee Vining on Hwy 395, a sign that reads; Lundy Canyon. The first trailhead is located at 7,730 feet just left of the Lundy Lake Dam. This trail will rise in elevation following the south side of Lundy Lake to Lake Canyon. It only took us only four days to complete this loop which will end at the Lundy Canyon Campground.

I shared this adventure with my hiking partners, Clem Bingham and Fred Cochran. We followed this old abandoned wagon road south to Oneida Lake at the base of the historic Lundy Mine area. This old wagon road was deteriorated over time but was much easier to follow than expected. Hard to believe along the road a few original telegraph poles were still standing since the 1870's. The final two hundred yards of trail was overgrown on each side with tall ground cover, but opened up just below a lower mine shaft of modern day Crystal Mine.

We sat up our first campsite at Oneida Lake at 9,735 feet. Interestingly, the Oneida Lake water was held in place by a wooden log dam. This location was ideal for us to explore the discarded rusted mining equipment left over from the 1930's. During that time the Crystal Mining Company purchased the May Lundy Mine. They set up operations to rework the tailings from the surrounding mines and especially the May Lundy Mine. Originally the May Lundy Mine began

May Lundy Mine lodge for miners to eat and relax.
All that remains today is the stone structure on the mountain side.

Heavy equipment left from the Crescent Mining Co
after digging through the original tailings around 1933.

in 1878 and during its 20 years of production over $2,000,000.00 dollars in gold was extracted at $14.90 per ounce. Compared to 2016 price of gold per ounce at around $1,225.00, the value would be $164,429,530 in 2016. (USD)

This was our second morning, and it was time to locate that switch back trail which led up to the May Lundy Mine at 10,700 feet. In the beginning, this trail was difficult to follow because of the loose scree and tailings at the lower elevation. Once beyond that point, the trail was identifiable and easy to follow. A few of the wooden A-Frame structures supporting the ore car cables located on the mountainside were still standing.

Even though the wooden cabins that offered lodging and cooking facilities to the miners had deteriorated, their stone foundations still existed. Above this satellite area was the May Lundy Mine named after one of William Lundy's four daughters. From this point, there was

Photo from Dore Pass, 13,100 feet. Looking down on Ada (9998 feet) and Oneida (9,722 feet) Lakes located in Lundy Canyon.

This is a wooden dam on Oneida Lake used in mining operations.

no visible trail to the mine. I recommend only continuing if you are a seasoned hiker or climber. The steep angle and loose scree made the final ascent to the mine very difficult. But the personal rewards of the five-hour adventure overshadowed all the obstacles.

The following day we increased our campsite's elevation to 10,000 feet at Ada Lake in preparation to climb Dore Pass at 11,300 feet the next morning. In 1881 this historic route connected Lundy and the Bennettville mining areas. One had to take into consideration that the Tioga Pass Road wasn't constructed then. The miners only had trails to bring in their supplies. Dore Pass was not only for moving men and supplies back and forth but also heavy equipment. The "Homer Mining Index" described moving 16,000 pounds of equipment nine miles with 4,000 feet of elevation gain on this route in the winter of 1882. This task took 12 men, one mile of rope, with winches over two months to complete by using wooden sleds. The heaviest load was 4,200 pounds, which was transported on a wooden sled in the dead of winter. Now consider it only took the three of us in July under five hours to complete this adventure over Dore Pass to Saddlebag Lake. One has to feel respect for these miners over a century ago for their efforts in trying to become successful under those extreme conditions.

That same day, we descended to Saddlebag Lake at 10,090 feet and once again started climbing, but this time hiking the Lundy Pass trail toward Lundy Pass at 10,300 feet. This was a much gentler scenic pass that skirted around Hummingbird, Odell, Shamrock, and Helen Lakes. Our final campsite was at 10,100 feet below Helen Lake, the beginning of Mill Creek. The next morning we prepared for our final 1000-foot descent following Mill Creek to the Lundy Trailhead. Two highlights along this remote trail were the 50-foot Lundy Falls and our first view of the huge beaver dams that follow this water source. Another point of interest along the road to the Lundy campground was a large portrait in vibrant colors of an Indian Chief in full headdress on a huge 18-foot boulder that someone painted decades ago. No one knows who or when this work of art was completed, but it offered a change of atmosphere on the long four-mile dusty road.

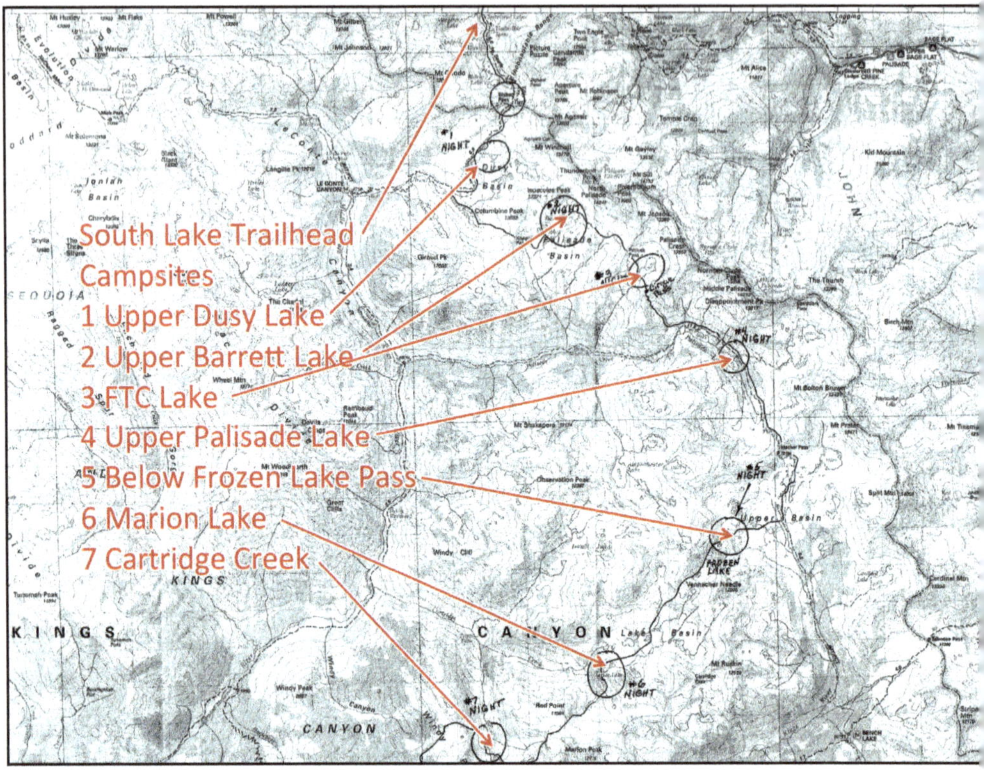

South Lake Trailhead
Campsites
1 Upper Dusy Lake
2 Upper Barrett Lake
3 FTC Lake
4 Upper Palisade Lake
5 Below Frozen Lake Pass
6 Marion Lake
7 Cartridge Creek

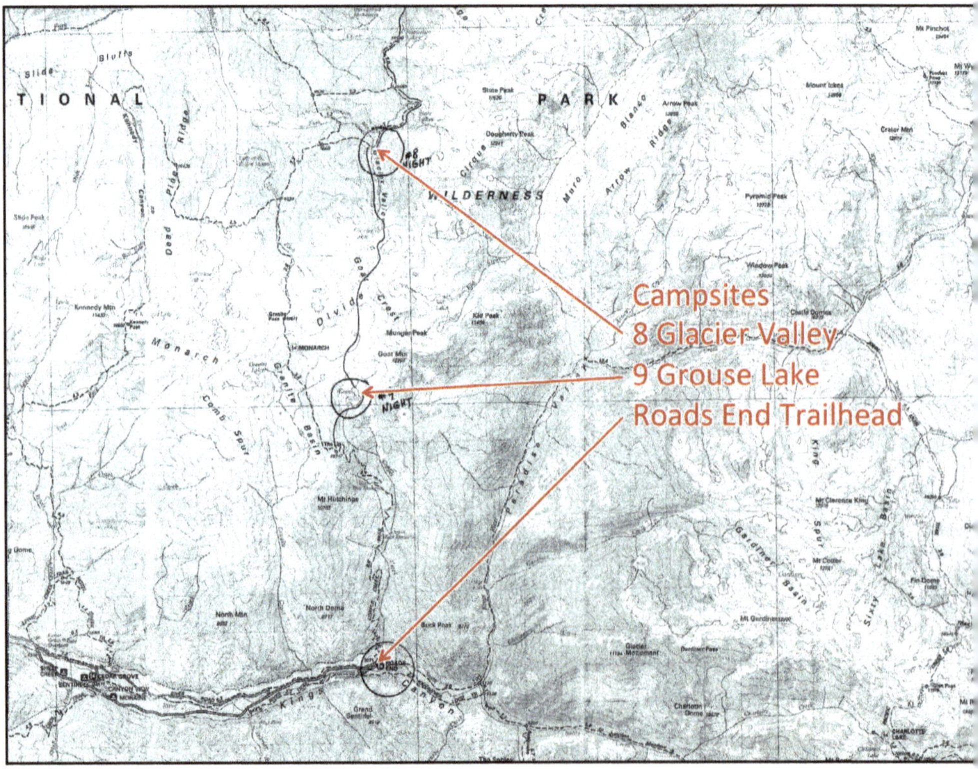

Campsites
8 Glacier Valley
9 Grouse Lake
Roads End Trailhead

Eighteen
High Sierra Route
August 05, 2008

Clem, Fred, and I spent most of the winter months researching material trying to find a moderate to strenuous cross-country route hiking across the top of the Sierra Mountains. After reading Steve Roper's book, High Sierra Route, the three of us were inspired by his five separate adventures across the high elevation passes and we decided on a 57 mile trek between South Lake outside of Bishop California on the east side. We concluded the adventure at Roads End within Kings Canyon National Park.

Our only major adjustment was the additional weight of packing 10 to 12 days of food on our back. We climbed over 11 remote passes, some reaching more than 12,000 feet.

The following July, we departed Oakhurst at two a.m. for the five-hour drive to Bishop California. At 8:15 A.M. we arrived at the South Lake Trailhead at 9,800 feet. That day we hiked eight miles over Bishop Pass at 11,972 feet. Then dropped down the opposite side to 11,300 feet to set up our first campsite at Dusy Basin.

The dark clouds that lingered overhead most of the afternoon gave up their moisture and from 5 to 7 p.m. we were confined to our tents. After dinner, I crawled into my sleeping bag around 9:00 p.m. and was ready for a night of sleep. At 2 a.m. I heard footsteps outside my tent. When I pulled back the tent flap, whatever it was had disappeared into the night. Twenty minutes later I heard those same

Potluck Pass 12,173 feet.

footsteps again. This time, he gave his personally away when he began to purr. The Mountain Lion was probably checking out the intruders camped within his personal territory.

From this point, there were no established trails. All that I could see in front of me were lots of various sizes of rocks. Off in the distance between two peaks was Knapsack Pass at 11,673 feet. This moderate climb took us to our second campsite located on a huge shelf at Barrett Lake. At this elevation, there were no trees, just a few isolated bushes and lots of rocks. The lake was nestled against a towering mountain reaching up more than 12,600 feet.

The following morning our objective was a south-facing slope for an 800-foot elevation gain to Potluck Pass. Our destination was a no-name lake at 11,676 feet. This area's lake was the start of Glacier Creek and was one of our highest campsites during the adventure. Nighttime temperatures dropped down to almost freezing which was expected at those elevations. Once the sun rose over the eastern mountains, it was only a short duration of time before the 50-degree temperature could be expected.

We repeated the boulder hopping technique as practiced the previous day. Cirque Pass at 12,100 feet was our next destination. This pass was rated as another strenuous climb. Once again we used handholds. The difficulty of trying to balance ourselves with a full pack was our main concern. I appreciated those large boulders that made excellent handholds. Once at the saddle, looking at the other side, I realized we had to descend another 1,487 feet to the John Muir Trail. We got a break and followed an established trail instead of the guessing game of boulder hoping.

As difficult as my explanation may state, once we reached the saddle, the views were almost unexplainable. Looking back on the

Looking at the Great Western Divide from Gray Crest Saddle.

route were the valleys and canyons dotted with remote mountain lakes nestled into rugged canyons. A few of those mountain peaks were still dressed in their winter coat of white. Looking forward into the next huge valley were the two Palisades Lakes that the John Muir Trail skirted around. Our next campsite would be the Upper Lake next to a 12-foot waterfall.

Mather Pass would be much easier following the gentle switchback trail to its 12,080-foot pass. Mather Pass was named after Stephen Tyng Mather (1867-1930) first director of the National Park Service. Once again, the reward was the summit following our climb. Looking back at the Palisades Lakes from this elevation focused in on the depth and size of the enormous valley. On the opposite side looking into the valley at 11,350 feet was the Upper Basin. This basin formed the glacial lakes that created the headwaters of the South Fork of the Kings River. Even this picturesque basin with its small lakes was overshadowed by the surrounding mountains. The peaks were over 13,000 feet and were still displaying their blanket of snow from the previous winter.

The Muir Trail descended into the basin and was the easiest route before starting our cross-country trek toward Frozen Lake Pass at 12,350 feet. We set our campsite at the base of this pass for an early start the following morning. Before starting this adventure, our research stated that Frozen Lake Pass was rated as the steepest pass along this 57-mile route. It was a sloping pass with stacks of huge granite pieces that broke loose from the mountain face. The 60-degree angle of climb extended more than 300 feet. Once again the views were spectacular from the narrow four foot wide flat called a saddle.

During our descent, all I could think about was walking on part of the old abandoned John Muir Trail, which was rerouted in 1938. After skirting around those lower lakes in this valley, we hiked toward the southern mountain range, and we crossed this lost trail. We set our sights for Marion Lake before we lost our daylight. Dropping down off of a narrow shelf into a forested canyon, next to a creek was a crumbled small log cabin. Could this be one of Shorty Loveless trapping cabins? Shorty Loveless was a fur trapper that made his living

Frozen Lake Pass on the right.

during the winter from 1910 to 1952 in these mountains.

After 12 hours of hiking, we arrived at Marion Lake. This lake was named after Marion Licanto, wife of Joseph LeConte Jr., the first president of The Sierra Club. His father was Joseph LeConte (1823-1901) he was a Professor of geology and natural history for the University of California. The LeConte Memorial Lodge in Yosemite National Park was also dedicated to him in 1904.

Legend had it that she and her husband were frequent visitors to the lake during the late 1800's. Although she died in 1924, two years later a memorial plaque was mounted on a granite boulder on the west shore. It catches the first rays of sun peaking over the mountain every morning.

The following day we climbed Red Pass at 11,600 feet and White Pass at 11,700 feet. Today's trek was successful by following game tracks. I have always stated that if one is confused on directions, just look for animal tracks. They will find the easiest direction from point A to point B. After following their tracks, we set our sights toward our next campsite, Cartridge Creek.

The following morning we dropped in elevation to Gray Pass at 11,000 feet and Horseshoe Lakes at 10,858 feet. At this point, we intersected a trail that led us to Glacier Valley Creek our lowest elevation campsite at 9,960 feet. I would classify this campsite as our most exciting of the adventure. Snuggled within the trees, the local deer had no fear of us. Twice they almost walked through our campsite on their journey to the creek.

We climbed over our final two passes, Goat Crest Saddle at 11,480 feet and Grouse Lake Pass at 11,050 feet. Looking down at Grouse Lake 1,000 feet below us was our final campsite.

Sitting around the camp that evening Clem, Fred, and I compared our memorable experiences we shared in the last nine days. I wasn't the only one who had mixed emotions knowing this adventure was coming to an end. But seriously, we were looking forward to hot showers and a soft clean bed to sleep in the following evening.

Morning came quickly and before long we were trekking through our last mile of cross-country looking to intersect the Copper Creek Trail. This trail dropped in elevation over 5,000 feet to our trailhead at Roads End in Kings Canyon National Park.

Before we completed our final day, along this last trail, a Black Bear bid us farewell. He looked at us from the top of a Sugar Pine Tree along the trail. Lucky for us his main focus was on a Sugar Pine Cone extended at the far end of one of the tree's branches. He eventually climbed down from his lofty perch and crossed our trail in front of us, but continued up the mountain totally ignoring us. Hard to believe that during our ten days hiking across these mountains, this was the only bear encounter.

Nineteen
North Lake, Piute Pass and Beyond
July 25, 2009

  This adventure began outside of Bishop, California, on the east side of the Sierra Nevada Mountains. The trailhead started at North Lake, less than one hour's drive west of Bishop. Our final destination could be considered a loop finishing at Rock Creek Lake just above Mosquito Flat Trail Camp. Only 48 miles were shown on our map for this High Route across the top of the mountains. Joining me again were my hiking partners Clem Bingham and Fred Cochran.

  The North Lake trailhead started at 9,360 feet. This trail followed Bishop Creek as it flowed from the higher elevation lakes. Our objective was to hike to one of the lakes beyond Piute Pass at 11,423 feet. As we climbed in elevation, the tall trees and thick ground cover were becoming victims of the altitude change. The trees were much shorter, and the ground cover became thinner. On a positive note, this landscape has opened up to reveal hidden waterfalls and interesting rock formations.

  The first major lake along the route was Loch Leven Lake at 10,740 feet. A local hiker told me that these series of lakes were excellent trout fishing. With its lack of trees, Piute Lake at 10,958 feet will reflect the same landscaping. This was another long mountain lake with ideal campsites or just a scenic resting place for those weary hikers.

Tony and Fred descending from Puppet Pass 11,800 feet.

Piute Pass was the first of several mountain passes we experienced during the six-day adventure. Two hikers passed us as we struggled hiking toward the saddle. I spoke with one few of them carrying only a daypack, and he stated that this popular trail had become a weekend adventure. We even had to give the right-of-way to a mule packer taking supplies into one of the Golden Trout Lakes. When we reached the saddle of Piute Pass we met the same packer on his return heading back to the corral. Maybe for future hikes we should consider traveling by horse or mule, one can cover twice the distance in the same allotted time.

Next we hiked around Summit Lake that was hosting a group of excited Boy Scouts. We later were informed they were an inner city troupe, and this was their first adventure into the mountains. Summit Lake was too busy for us to spend the night. So we decided to continue hiking beyond the point of departing from the trail and look at Tomahawk Lake. We paused and after looking at our map, we decided to hike another hour and set up our first campsite at Lower Desolation Lake at 11,120 feet. The name was appropriate for its description; the landscaping consisted of rocks and boulders with the lack of any vegetation.

Looking up at the dark clouds forming over the western mountains, could it be possible that we get a thundershower before dark? Twenty minutes after setting up camp we had our first mountain shower. After an hour the sky cleared, introducing millions of stars resembling diamonds spread over a black velvet cloth. While gazing at the sky that evening I said to myself, "This spectacle of nature is only reserved for those who dare to climb into these mountains."

Looking up at Piute Pass, 11,423 feet, from trail around lake.

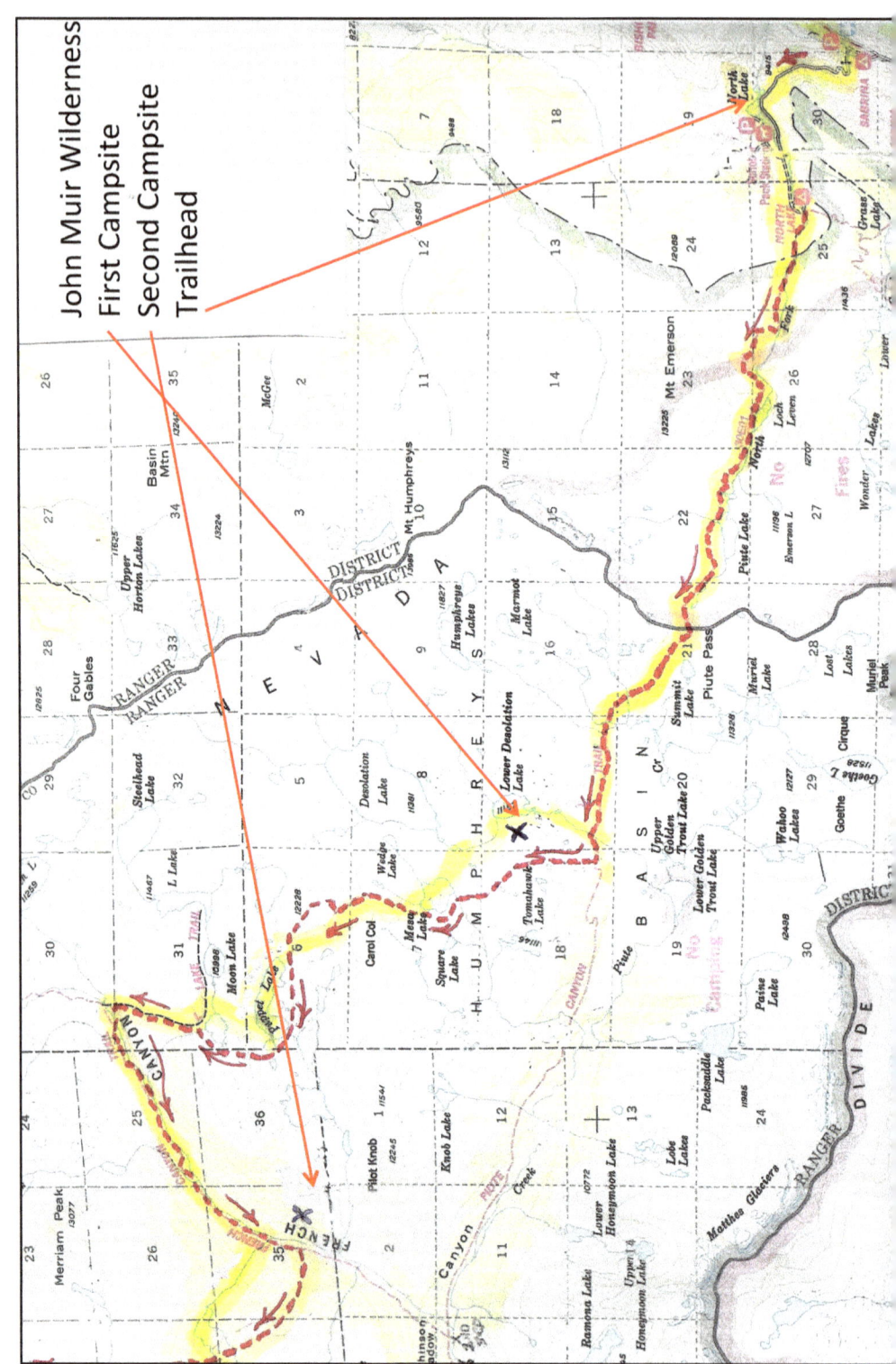

Twenty
Surprises at Puppet Pass and LaSalle Lake
July 26, 2009

Day two and we awoke to clear skies with not a trace of yesterday's thunderstorm clouds. Mesa Lake at 11,350 feet was our next reference point before the challenge of Puppet Pass. After reading Steve Roper's book, High Sierra Route, we wanted to see for ourselves if those words printed within his book described this remote route.

As expected during this ascent we climbed over huge boulders (called talus) and finally we reached the saddle at 11,800 feet. Looking behind us, in the distance was the rugged mountain range called Glacier Divide. Even during midsummer, those mountains were still displaying snow snuggled within their canyons. We followed along its range yesterday from Piute Pass before hiking cross-country toward our campsite at Desolation Lake. Piute Pass or can be spelled Paiute was named after the American Indians of the Owens Valley a branch of the Shoshone family.

North West from Puppet Pass, the distant view of this huge valley was nestled between mountains over 13,000 feet. The pristine valley cradled many natural mountain lakes. One major lake was Puppet Lake, which was part of our journey this day. Gazing out across the huge valley and on the opposite side of Puppet Lake was a towering mountain face. It rose in elevation over 200 feet boarding the lakes shoreline. The feature that caught my eye was a small ribbon of water cascading down

Fred and Tony forging through snow above LaSalle Lake toward Feather Pass 12,375 feet.

over two hundred feet from the plateau above into the lakes surface. Wow, this view related closely to the spectacle when entering Yosemite Valley. From our vantage point, Puppet Lake resembled a hand puppet.

Surprises came when descending down the north pass face. I would classify this descent as class three, difficult but challenges one's skills descending to the valley floor 570 feet below. During this steep descent we were clinging to any anchored object to help support each maneuver dropping into the valley. While walking around the lakes, I wondered if the trout were biting. I saw them rising and feeding off the surface. I'll never know because my fishing gear was at home.

Next, we dropped down two major shelves, searching for the Pine Creek Pass Trail. Once we found the trail, we knew eventually it would cross two major run-off streams. Next was the junction of the major French Canyon Trail, which we followed to our next campsite.

The time was around one o'clock, and again we were threatened with dark clouds and the possibility of rain, lightning, and thunder. Looked like I'd use my rain gear before reaching the junction of French Canyon and Merriam Lake Trail.

Mountain Secrets Revealed

The rain and thunder continued off and on during the evening, but around eight o'clock the rain stopped and allowed us time to cook our evening meal. We weren't alone! Our uninvited visitors were small and were interested in our bare skin. Yes, the uninvited guests were mosquitoes. They forced us to eat inside our tents that evening.

Day three started early, and we began our 800 feet ascension to Merriam Lake. The lake and Merriam Peak at 13,077 feet were named after Doctor Clinton Hart Merriam (1865-1942) in 1929 by the California State Geographic Board.

After the first 500 feet, we crossed a beautiful long green meadow. Circling its northern border was a wide run-off stream flowing from the lake above. On the opposite side, we started climbing through a slot for our final 300 feet of elevation. Maybe I could call this climb a class 3 trail.

Looking from Puppet Pass, 11,800 feet, to Puppet Lake and the French Canyon Trail at 10,660 feet.

Finally we arrived at Merriam Lake, a moderate size mountain lake surrounded by boulders nestled within a small canon. At the far end of this Lake, an inlet stream cascaded down 290 feet along the pathway to our next campsite. Once again there was no trail to LaSalle Lake at 11,562 feet. Once we reached the top, we forged across two hundred yards of snow before crossing the run off stream to search for a personal campsite along the Lake.

Again we encountered rain and thunder along with the added excitement of hail the size of a coin (penny). We took up shelter under an overhanging rock until the hail turned into rain. At around 9:10 that evening our attention was focused on the sound of thunder, followed by a prolonged thunder roll, which resembled the noise of a freight train. Would you believe the mountain behind us decided to give way and started a landslide tumbling toward the lake below? We were in no danger, but it sure made me think, what if our campsite was in a different location? When the first rays of light struck the mountain crest the next morning, we saw the darkened area where part of the mountain slipped away.

Twenty-one
Feather Pass to Lake Italy
July 28, 2009

It was early morning on day four as we started our 813-foot climb to Feather Pass. With the excitement of the landslide last evening, first light revealed the remaining darkened area after its surface rocks slid into the lake. Just in case the mountain decided to add a repeat performance, the three of us packed up early, skirted around the lake and started our climb at the northern end.

Each pass had its own personality. They demanded your respect, but it was your choice to find the safest route and follow with caution until reaching your objective. Feather Pass was much easier as compared to Puppet Pass but personally one forgets the difficulties once reaching the top. After gazing at the distant views, the spectacle of the surrounding mountains and valleys helps one forget the hardships.

Feather Pass was named after the rock formations along the crest that resembled the Feathered Head Dress of our American Indians. Once again we forged our way through snow in three separate areas on the east slope. At the mountain base, we hiked around the small bodies of water created by snow run-off called Tarns. These bodies of water were smaller than a lake but larger than a pond.

Bear Paw Lake was our next objective, which in 1952 was named by Elden H. Vestal of the DFG (Department of Fish and Game) survey party. There were more than 20 lakes in this recess and

Lake Italy at 11,200 feet looking toward Mt. Julius Caesar at 13,206 feet.

thirteen of them had bear related names. But keep in mind we had no sighting of a bear, and there has never been a report of a bear episode connected with any of these lakes. We dropped down to 11,500 feet before hiking around the northern shoreline of Bear Paw Lake. This long lake gave us a great perspective of shadows reflecting from the surrounding mountains as the sun set in the western sky.

Ursa Lake was another large lake at almost the same elevation. Our next campsite was on its rare grassy northern shoreline. This picturesque lake was one of our utmost scenic camps. Its backdrop to the south was the Seven Gables Mountains towering at 13,160 feet. Behind us in the small grassy canyon, a steep granite wall extended upward over 200 feet. Closer inspection reveals a climbing slot for our departure the following morning. The reflection off this lake was breathtaking that evening during the color changes at sunset. Ursa Lake was also named in 1952 by Elden H. Vestal working with the DFG

Ursa Lake at 11,502 feet with the Seven Gables Peaks at 13,160 in the background. Our three tents in the foreground.

survey group. The Seven Gables peaks were named on September 20, 1894, by Theodore S. Solomon's and Leigh Bierce.

One positive point about the higher elevations, the mosquito population had almost disappeared, so we ate outside our tents. Once again we had light rain showers, which developed a brilliant light display from the moisture held within the dark clouds. The setting sun also created a reddish afterglow. A few clouds produced a fiery orange display against the dark colored background of the night sky. What a light show to witness from that elevation.

Day five and we started climbing the 200-foot slot that led us to Black Bear Lake and circled around a few larger tarns. Another half mile to White Bear Lake at 11,750 feet, then to our next saddle called White Bear Pass at 11,800 feet.

Then we started our descent to Brown Bear Lake at 11,150 feet and Teddy Bear Lake at 10,900 feet. This group of professional survivors must have loved bears! Our map kept us sane following this collection of bear names. Now you know why hikers carry those small pills called Ibuprofen!

Looking northwest in the distance was Mount Helgard at 13,361 feet. Directly in front of this mountain was Helgard Canyon, which brought back personal memories from August 30, 1992. That was the date when I first solo hiked to Lake Italy from the Bear Creek Trailhead.

If we followed this canyon west, it would lead us to the John Muir Trail. But we hiked east toward Lake Italy to our next campsite. Once reaching the lake at 11,202 feet we found an ideal shelter along the east shoreline. Someone had stacked up stones three feet high to deflect the wind as it blew up the canyon at night. Lake Italy was named by the USGS (United States Geographical Survey) during the 1907-1909 survey because it had the vague resemblance of a boot or the shape of Italy.

Then reality became disappointment, Clem accidentally lost his tent somewhere during our seven miles of cross-country hiking. Clem and I backtracked over two miles without any success. We figured he must have lost his tent descending off of White Bear Pass. It must have torn loose or was snagged by the thick Willow Bushes on the mountainside. Trying to find his direct route without the assistance of a marked trail would be impossible. We returned back to camp without his tent.

Luckily we had an extra tarp, rope, wooden clothes pins, bungee cords and ingenuity so Clem had shelter for the reminder of our trip. That evening we had another repeat performance of thunder, lightning, and rain showers. We had our dinner inside our tents again.

The next day we'd hike over Cox Col Pass, which would be our highest pass at 13,040 feet. If all worked out during the final climb, we would be at the trailhead the following day.

Twenty-two
Mystery of Cox Col Pass
July 30, 2009

Today started day six and our climb over Cox Call Pass. After five days of afternoon rain and thundershowers, maybe our luck would change. Clear skies in the morning as we started the climb to 13,040 feet. First, we crossed Lake Italy's run-off stream and then followed the north shoreline for over a mile before reaching the lake's eastern boundary. High mountain peaks surrounded the picturesque lake. To the east was Mount Julius Caesar at 13,196 feet, named by Alfred H. and Myrtle Prater, who in 1928 made the first ascent to its summit. Its name came about by its proximity to Lake Italy. To the north was Mount Abbot at 13,704 feet, and Mount Gabb at 13,711 feet. Mount Abbot, named by the Whitney Survey in 1864 for Henry Larcom Abbot (1831-1927), a soldier and engineer. Mount Gabb was also named by the Whitney Survey in 1862 for William More Gabb (1839-1878), a paleontologist. Before reaching the lake we hiked past Mount Hilgard at 13,361 feet. Mount Hilgard was named after Eugene Woldemar Hilgard (1833-1916), a professor of agriculture.

This morning we passed only one small mountain lake called Toe Lake. Do you think someone must have been thinking of a humorous name? What part of the foot was at the front end of a boot? This proper name fit the location of this lake, which was located at the front of the historic shape of Lake Italy.

Looking down from Cox Col Pass 13,040 feet. This pass defeated us and we had a three day detour toward Mosquito Flat Trailhead. Trailhead located within the cluster of trees at photo background.

Without realizing, we climbed a difficult route until almost 12,600 feet. At this point we were faced with a horizontal move across the face just below the summit. For the next two hours we boulder hopped over large talus (large boulders) and one questionable section of loose scree (small gravel). With each step, the mountain surface kept slipping toward the valley below. When I finally decided to rest and sat down on a huge three-ton boulder, it started to move and slid over fifteen feet before coming to rest against another hunk of granite below me. Even the larger talus was not stable at this extreme angle. Hiking over the patches of snow offered some relief from the continuous boulder hopping. Finally after five hours, we reached the final plateau and in the distance was the saddle of Cox Col Pass.

At the pass, we were in for a surprise. We had a choice of three separate routes descending to the valley floor. The map rated this pass as class 2, but ropes hanging on the mountainside added confusion. Did someone make a mistake when classifying this pass? Between us we arrived at a unanimous decision. We agreed that with the snow and steepness of the south face, this pass was much too dangerous to continue. We'd have to look for an alternate route to the trailhead in the valley below.

During the time span of researching our map, a repeat performance by those thick dark clouds was gathering overhead. Thunder, lightning, and rain found us again that afternoon. We decided to double back down to the lower plateau at 12,200 feet and set up a campsite next to the snow run-off. There we could further research our map for an alternate route to Mosquito Flat Trailhead.

The only route into the valley where our vehicle was located was called the Piute Trail, but this established trail would increase our hiking time another three days. Luckily we had enough food between us to complete this alternate route.

The rain clouds moved out around eight o'clock that evening. The sky opened up to another beautiful arrangement of diamonds spread out on a black velvet cloth. At that elevation, the sky was crystal clear introducing each star and constellation. We saw the Milky Way, Orion, Big and Little Dipper just to mention a few familiar nighttime symbols. What a treat to lie there at 12,200 feet and gaze upon our solar system without any obstructions.

After researching our map for an alternate route, we decided to hike north over Gabbot Pass at 12,250 feet. Then we followed the run-off stream as it cascaded through a gently angled drainage toward the Second Recess.

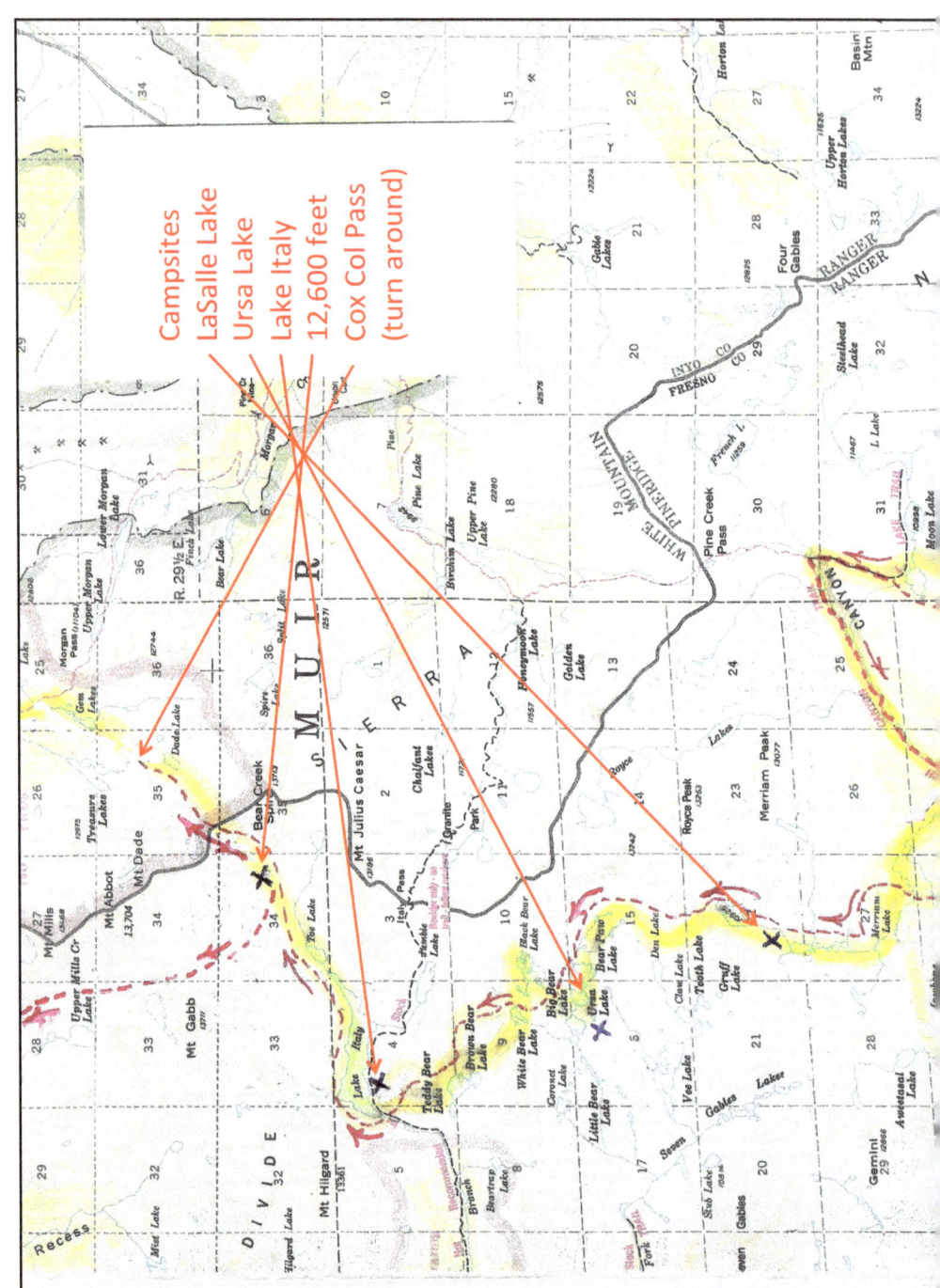

Twenty-three
Detour into Mountain History
July 31, 2009

Day seven was a different experience starting this morning next to a snow bank on the rock shelf at 12,200 feet. In the night, the crystal clear sky dropped the temperature below freezing and caused a layer of ice to form on our tents. Maybe today we'd be spared the thunder and lightning associated with the last few days. Looking south from this mountain shelf, off in the distance below us was the mile long Lake Italy at 11,202 feet. To our west was Gabbot Pass at 12,250 feet along our destination for today's journey. We'd drop another 200 feet into a small ravine before starting our climb toward this mountain saddle.

After completing the alternate pass, we followed the canyon as it dropped 3,700 feet through the Second Recess toward Trail Camp at 8,500 feet. This new detour added another eighteen miles, three extra days, and two new mountain passes to our adventure. Looking at the positive side of this alternate adventure, we'd be following the old Mono Trail over Mono Pass, which the American Indians used for centuries trading goods with their eastern brothers.

It was difficult to believe that some of the higher elevation lakes were visited by Sea Gulls. Not large numbers, just a few looking for that tasty trout for morning breakfast. For the first time in all of my adventures, ravens soared above 12,000 feet, riding the thermals like our native birds of prey.

After dropping down off the first pass, we started following this long canyon with its many tarns created by the melting snow. The natural stream between those tarns offered an excellent path as it twisted and turned then fell to the canyon below. The day would be another afternoon of boulder hopping before entering the tree line.

Later that morning, climbing toward us were two hikers whose objective was to climb over the pass that defeated us the previous day. They informed us that it was their third experience hiking over Cox Cal Pass. After a brief conversation, they explained the route over the pass was to the extreme west of the area we examined. They aroused my curiosity and agreed to exchange emails and send me a map outlining this so-called class two route.

At the junction of the second and third recess, off in the distance was the natural landmark called Hart Cave. This natural cave entrance was heart shaped and easily recognized from our distant vantage point.

We descended over eight miles before reaching our final obstacle, which was Mono Creek. When we think of creeks, we picture small streams that can be jumped or boulder hopped across. We were in for a surprise, that small stream was a raging torrent of water over thirty feet wide. An hour passed as we searched its bank before realizing there was no shallow crossing. Maybe there was no way to cross without getting wet. So I started retracing our footsteps and looking for any object in this area that was out of place. Fred challenged himself and tried forging his way through the thick foliage looking for a safe crossing downstream. After twenty minutes he found his way back to the trail, disappointed.

Meantime during my search, I noticed an area that the native grass was trampled and a few small broken bush branches leading away from the trail. After a few minutes of breaking my own branches following this makeshift path, it led to a fallen tree that extended across the creek. Not a very large diameter tree but large enough to attempt a crossing. We challenged our balancing skills and make a successful crossing. Lucky we made that decision because this natural bridge was the only dry crossing leading us to the Mono Trail.

Campsite at Mono Creek along the Mono Trail. My surprise birthday party in the wilderness. Hikers know how to enjoy themselves!!

To my surprise on the opposite side of Mono Creek was the Trail Junction Camp, our designated campsite for the night. Next to this camp was the major junction of the Mono Trail, which we followed the next morning on our quest over Mono Pass.

Another surprise was waiting for me that evening when I returned from the creek with water for cooking. Someone had decorated my tent with bright colored posters expressing, Happy Birthday! Fred and Clem surprised me by remembering that August the first was another milestone in my life. Also concealed within their packs were a couple of bottles, which I call the nectar of the gods to help celebrate the occasion. With the forethought of my friends, we celebrated my birthday at 8,500 feet in the Sierra Nevada Wilderness, next to the historic Mono Trail. Wow! What a birthday surprise!

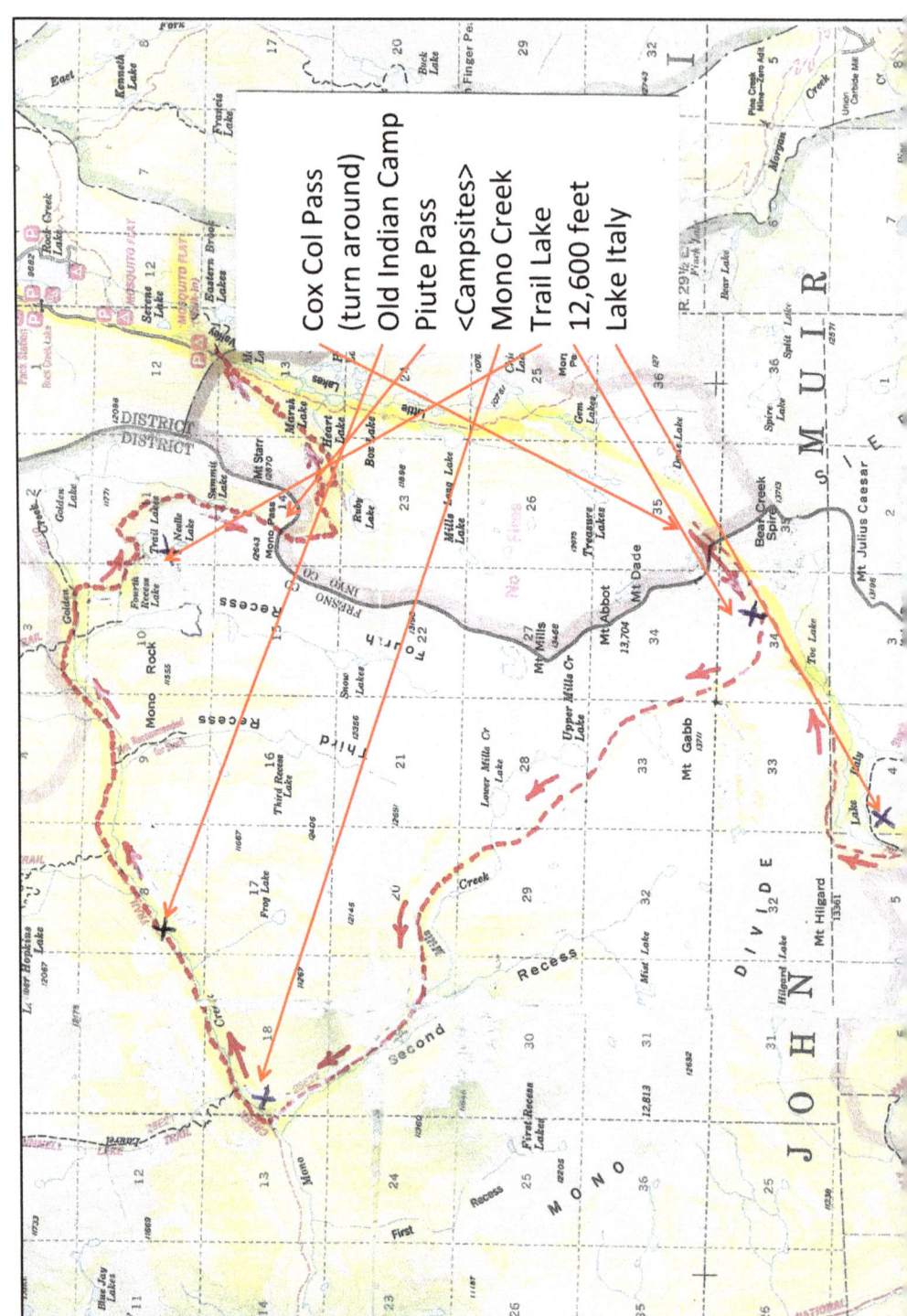

Twenty-four
History along the Mono Trail
August 01, 2009

It's been since July 14, 1986, that I hiked part of the historic trail to Grinnell Lake. I shared that adventure with the famous mountain man and hiker Tom Addison or as most knew him, the Silver Fox.

Today Clem, Fred, and I hiked that famous trail to the eastern side of the Sierra Nevada Mountains. We would need one last campsite that evening if we couldn't complete the 3,545 feet of elevation gain to Mono Pass.

Since this was a well-traveled trail, the junction points were marked with trail signs identifying area locations. The first was Grinnell Lake at 10,804 feet named after Professor Joseph Grinnell in 1940. The second junction was the trail to Lower Hopkins Lake at 10,354 feet and Upper Hopkins Lake at 11,082 feet, named after Mark Hopkins during the 1907-09 surveys.

We had hiked eight miles along the Second Recess from Gabbot Pass. Other junction points were the Third and Forth Recess. Each of those canyons offered excellent hiking opportunities into the higher elevation lakes.

One skill I developed over the years was recognizing old American Indian Camps. I got lucky when I ventured off the trail and located a camp with obsidian chips still visible on the surface.

Surveyor's Cabin along Mono Trail at 12,000 feet.

Continuing up the trail, just before the Forth Recess was another high elevation historic land mark called Mono Rock. This huge hunk of granite extended skyward to an elevation of 11,555 feet. At the base of the Forth Recess was the Forth Recess Lake, surrounded on three sides by the steep cliffs and fronted by pine and cedar trees. After five hours of hiking we crossed another large stream, which was the run-off from Golden Lake, another high elevation lake offering excellent Golden Trout fishing.

When the sun started setting into the western horizon, we realized that Mono Pass would have to wait until the next morning. Before six o'clock we arrived at Trail Lake our location for camping that night. Huge boulders surrounded the lake and offered an excellent windbreak from the chilly winds that blew up the mountain canyon. On the west end of the lake was a stone survivor's cabin. It was abandoned and locked for safety purposes. The date etched in the concrete around the steps read 1948. For my own curiosity, I stepped off the cabins dimensions of 20 X 30 feet. Today our satellites replaced the survivors

Tony hiking toward Mono Pass at 12,642 feet.

from physical hiking over the mountains to document range and township lines.

We awakened to another beautiful morning with the sun peeking over the eastern mountains. It was August second, and we were looking forward to completing our adventure before noon. One final hike followed a switchback trail toward a high elevation plateau. Summit Lake greeted us just before ascending to Mono Pass at 12,643 feet. We stopped at the pass and looked south toward the mountain range above us, which was the location of Cox Col Pass. With my field glasses, I could see why the ropes were attached to the mountain wall. Cox Col was a very steep pass and our lack of research forced us into our detour down to the Mono Pass Trail.

Next, we passed Ruby Lake, which was very popular with the local day hikers being only three miles from the Mosquito Flat Trailhead. In our final miles today, we must have met fifty hikers escaping into the sanctuary of the wilderness.

We finally completed our cross-country adventure in nine days. It started out as a forty-eight-mile hike and was increased to fifty-

View from Mono Trail looking at Cox Col Pass between the two peaks.

five miles. By accepting a forced detour, our adventure was extended from six days to nine days. We mastered eight major passes and forged across many snow belts at elevations between 8,560 and 13,040 feet. I have only one single comment to share with all of you; I'm satisfied, but tired!

Twenty-five
P-40 Fourth of Fifth Found
September 29, 2016

Lieutenant John H. Pease was the first to have mechanical problems. He bailed out and survived touching ground somewhere around Kennedy Meadows. His bird remained a mystery for 75 years, possibly because of the remote area. I'm happy to say he is living in Colorado and almost 97 years old.

In June of this year a alone hiker; Jonathan Beck hiking along the South Fork of the Kern River found an aircraft wreckage. After confirming that this aircraft is Lieutenant John H. Pease's, Pat Macha (historian in identifying aircraft crash sites) set up a "Remembrance Mission" for September 18, 2016. On that date John Pease Jr; son of the pilot and six other adventures hiked to that location in tribute to his father.

Since Clem Bingham, Fred Cochran and I photographed three of those five P-40 crash sites, we decided to search that remote area of the Kern River and photograph Pease's crash site. On September 28, 2016 Clem and I departed for the trail head at Kennedy Meadows. Fred had previous family commitments and could not attend this adventure.

We departed from the Wildrose Trailhead at Kennedy Meadows. Hiking through this high desert location brings back memories of my early hiking adventures when I lived in Southern California. Sand, rocks, scrub brush and a few ancient Cedar and Pine Trees share the mountain sides. A large percentage of this aged trail follows through washes carved over time from the winter snow runoff. Sad these mountains still have the scars from previous fires that left just the charcoal remains of those proud centennials that once graced these mountain sides.

We set up our base camp a short distance from a natural spring still flowing with sweet cool water even in late September. We departed the following morning to search out the wreck site location. After hiking almost three miles through forgotten canyons and mountain passes we dropped into a remote valley. In the distance we could

P-40 engine block with manifold

see a plateau at 7,500 feet, which is our destination according to our GPS waypoints. Upon arrival once again we are the victims of wrong waypoints. After two hours of searching the general area we located the aircraft site. The sun reflecting off the aluminum revealed its location on a steep mountain side. Distance to the west was almost half mile off and to the north almost a quarter of a mile.

As we climbed the mountain side we encountered smaller aluminum pieces that washed down over time. Directly above us lying within the scrub brush was the mangled remains of the engine. Scattered in every direction was twisted and compressed aluminum pieces that varied in size. Roughly 50 feet above the engine was the crater where the airplane made contact with the mountain. Inside this 20 foot crater was only one of the three propeller blades still connected to the spinner mechanism.

Clem Bingham and me holding the prop blade.

Me holding the 50 caliber machine gun.

After 74 years four of the five aircraft that disappeared on October 24, 1941 have been identified. Only one remaining Curtiss Wright P-40 Tomahawk war bird is still hiding somewhere in Kings Canyon National Park. That was Lieutenant Leonard Lyden's #29-394 aircraft.

For those of you who are not familiar with this war bird, it gained fame defending China in 1941 with the "Flying Tigers". And that same year it defended Pearl Harbor on December 07, 1941.

Photo of me holding the prop blade.

www.ingramcontent.com/pod-product-compliance
Lightning Source LLC
Chambersburg PA
CBHW040329300426
44113CB00020B/2700